Intelligent IT Outsourcing:
Eight Building Blocks to Success

[signature]

Leslie Willcocks

Intelligent IT Outsourcing: Eight Building Blocks to Success

Sara Cullen
Leslie P. Willcocks

ELSEVIER
BUTTERWORTH
HEINEMANN

AMSTERDAM BOSTON HEIDELBERG LONDON NEW YORK OXFORD
PARIS SAN DIEGO SAN FRANCISCO SINGAPORE SYDNEY TOKYO

Other titles in the Series
Corporate politics for IT managers: how to get streetwise
Delivering IT and ebusiness value
eBusiness implementation
eBusiness strategies for virtual organizations
ERP: the implementation cycle
The effective measurement and management of IT costs and benefits
A hacker's guide to project management 2nd edition
How to become a successful IT consultant
How to manage the IT helpdesk 2nd edition
Information warfare: corporate attack and defence in a digital world
IT investment – making a business case
Knowledge management – a blueprint for delivery
Make or break issues in IT management
Making IT count
Managing in the Email Office
Network security
Prince 2: a practical handbook
The project manager's toolkit
Reinventing the IT department
Understanding the internet
Value-Driven IT Management

x

About the authors

Sara Cullen is a former National Partner at Deloitte Touche Tohmatsu and one of the most experienced practitioners regarding outsourcing in Asia Pacific. She has provided her expertise to 75+ organizations in over 80 projects covering over 45 business functions, with contract values up to $1 billion per annum.

Sara is widely published on the subject and is highly sought after as an expert commenter. She has written 16 best practice and research publications, been featured in 40+ articles, presented in 70+ major conferences, conducted seven major reviews for government, provided expert independent advice in Senate inquiries and conducted editorial reviews of outsourcing research performed by the Harvard Business School and the *Journal of Information Technology*.

Leslie P. Willcocks is Professor of Information Management and E-business at Warwick Business School. He is internationally acknowledged for his work on IT outsourcing, evaluation, management, organization and change. He holds visiting positions at AGSM, Melbourne and Erasmus universities and is Associate Fellow at Templeton College, Oxford, where he was previously Fellow and Reader. He has been Editor of the *Journal of Information Technology* for 13 years, and previously worked in management consulting for 11 years.

Leslie is co-author of 23 books and over 130 papers in journals such as *Harvard Business Review, Sloan Management Review, MISQE, California Management Review* and *Communications of the ACM*. He is a frequent keynote speaker, is regularly retained as advisor by major corporations and service providers, and has been expert witness to, for example, the Australian Senate on central government IT outsourcing, and to the US Congressional Committee on the US Internal Revenue Services.

Figures

Tables

Return this card today and enter £100 book draw

Select the subjects you'd like to receive information about, enter your email and mail address and freepost it back to us.

TECHNOLOGY

Architecture and Design:
- History of architecture ○
- Landscape ○
- Urban design ○
- Sustainable architecture ○
- Planning and design ○

☐ **Building and Construction**

☐ **Computing: Professional:**
- Communications ○
- Data Management ○
- Enterprise Computing ○
- IT Management ○
- Operating Systems ○

☐ **Computing: Beginner:**
- Computing ○
- Programming ○

☐ **Conservation and Museology**

☐ **Engineering:**
- Aeronautical Engineering ○
- Automotive Engineering ○
- Chemical Engineering ○
- Health & Safety ○
- Environmental Engineering ○
- Plant / Maintenance / Manufacturing ○
- Marine Engineering ○
- Materials Science & Engineering ○
- Mechanical Engineering ○
- Petroleum Engineering ○
- Quality ○

☐ **Electronics and Electrical Engineering:**
- Electrical Engineering ○
- Electronic Engineering ○
- Radio, Audio and TV Technology ○
- Computer Technology ○

☐ **Film, Television, Video & Audio:**
- Audio/Radio ○
- Post Production ○
- Lighting ○
- Theatre Performance ○
- Photography/Imaging ○
- Radio ○
- TV ○
- Film/TV/Video Production ○
- Journalism ○
- Multimedia ○
- Computer Graphics/ Animation ○
- Broadcast Management & Theory ○
- Broadcast & Communications Technology ○

☐ **Security**

MANAGEMENT
- ☐ Finance and Accounting
- ☐ Hospitality, Leisure and Tourism
- ☐ HR and Training
- ☐ Pergamon Flexible Learning
- ☐ Knowledge Management
- ☐ Management
- ☐ Marketing
- ☐ IT Management

Name: _____

Email address: _____

Mail address: _____

Postcode _____ Date _____

Please keep me up to date by ☐ email ☐ post ☐ both

Science & Technology Books, Elsevier Ltd. Registered Office: The Boulevard, Langford Lane, Kidlington, Oxon OX5 1GB. Registered number: 1982084

Jo Blackford

Data Co-ordinator

Elsevier

FREEPOST - SCE5435

Oxford

Oxon

OX2 8BR

Introduction

Information technology outsourcing (ITO), or the plethora of names under which it is also known (including contracting out, partnering, FM, co-sourcing and many others), is handing over IT activities and assets to third party management for monitored outcomes. ITO has outlived the five-year period typical of a management fad and is now regarded as a standard IT management tool. As such, global market revenues have increased from $US9 billion in 1990 to $US154 billion by 2004 and a projected $US190+ billion by 2006 (Kern *et al.*, 2002a). This compares with research company IDC's estimates for all outsourced services of £1200 billion by 2006.

Some more figures. Looking at the IT budget of the average corporation or government agency, Willcocks *et al.* (2002) reckoned that by the end of 2001 some 72% was still being spent on in-house IT, the rest on IT outsourcing, including 3% on business process outsourcing (BPO) and 3% on offshore out-sourcing. Extrapolating global trends, it is likely by 2005 for IT outsourcing to represent 33% of the average IT budget, with offshore outsourcing taking up another 10%, and BPO a further 15%. Other sources, as shown in Figure 0.1, reveal over half of organizations across the globe are outsourcing at least 20% of their IT budgets.

Thus the vast majority of organizations outsource some aspect of their IT services – this includes public and private sector organizations of all sizes across all industries (Cullen *et al.*, 2001). And this has been a rising trend. Some economies, like those of the UK and USA, have averaged a 15% plus increase per annum in supplier revenues across the 1995–2002 period. Outsourcing has enabled organizations to survive the pace of change in the new economy at a time when business activities need to be focused on the right activities and resources need to be kept lean and aligned with the core business. From late 2000, as economies moved into a more recessionary climate, a renewed emphasis on cost savings followed, with increased interest not just in ITO, but also in offshore and business process outsourcing as new sources of cost reduction. Indeed, in the storm-tossed IT years of 2001 and

We provide concepts and options, but do not provide detailed step-by-step 'instructions'. It is not a detailed procedure manual; rather it provides checklists, outlines, traps to avoid, and a structured way forward. In this book, there are different examples of how the tools and techniques are applied in practice. These different methods are intended, as there is no 'right' way to go through the outsourcing lifecycle, just general principles to apply and a general precedence and sequencing of activities.

Look at this framework as optional strategies and techniques that the organization can decide whether or not to adopt within outsourcing projects. Furthermore, although the information is presented sequentially in accordance with the lifecycle, the reality of the outsourcing process is that many activities are done in parallel and many are not necessarily conducted in the order presented due to the circumstances facing the organization. In effect, use what is appropriate when it is appropriate for the situation. However, to give the reader confidence, what we can say is that everything we have provided in this book has been tried and tested, and has been found to work effectively in numerous actual outsourcing deals – large and small, complex and simple.

Why the need for a building block approach?

Unfortunately, for organizations and suppliers alike, outsourcing initiatives are too often done in a disjointed manner, with different individuals or teams carrying out, independently, what in fact are, and need to be made, interrelated activities (Figure 0.2).

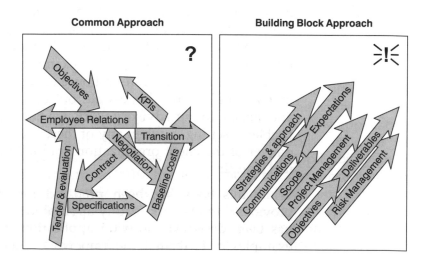

Figure 0.2
Streamlining the approach

For example, the CIO may determine the services to be outsourced, a legal team prepare the contract, an operational team prepare the SLAs, a separate team from all the above select the supplier, and a different team altogether formed to manage the supplier and so on.

We have observed that, in many cases, these teams have not fully understood the outcomes of the other teams' outputs and more importantly have not been privy to the debates and issue resolutions that took place to get there – thus lack a thorough understanding of the basis for the final arrangement. Furthermore, we have often seen that the outputs of the various teams overlap, at a minimum, and in the worst case can contradict each other.

Case Study: a utility

A state-base utility conducted what they believed to be a very cost effective tendering process that was slated to save the organization millions of dollars over a three-year period. Once the supplier selection was made, the individuals involved returned to their normal roles and the contract management team was formed from the previous in-house service delivery individuals who were, for various reasons, remaining within the organization. This team had no previous experience in tenders, contracts or supplier management. They needed to implement a rapid transition and ensure no disruptions to operations, so began working side-by-side with the supplier to ensure this occurred. Along the way, understandings, procedures and protocols were arranged between personnel in both parties that had little to do with the signed agreement. In fact, the field personnel in both parties had not read the agreement, although they had intended to once 'things quieted down'.

What resulted was a very different arrangement in practice than had been agreed, driven by the viewpoint of the contract management team as to what they believed worked best. As a result, services in scope were delivered by the organization rather than the supplier although they were included in the fee, new services included in the fee were never delivered, activities included in the monthly fee were also charged as out of scope, and only limited Key

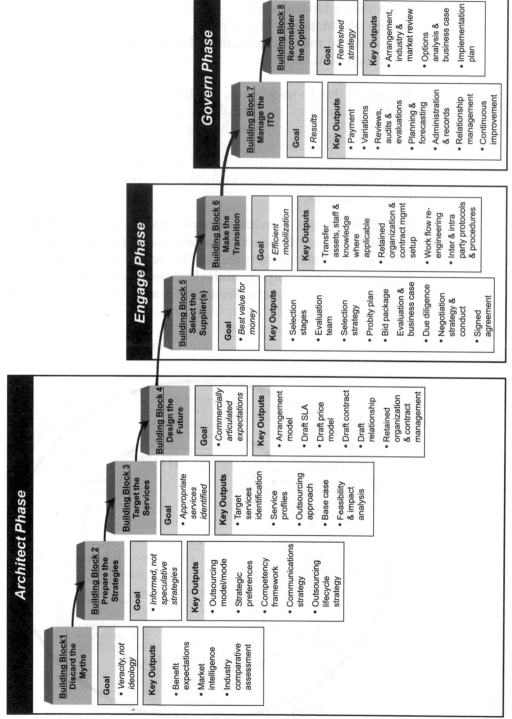

Figure 0.4 The outsourcing building block outputs

Part One

Architect Phase

The first building block – discard the myths: gather acumen

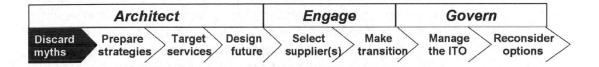

Architect			Engage		Govern	
Discard myths	Prepare strategies	Target services	Design future	Select supplier(s)	Make transition	Manage the ITO	Reconsider options

There are many misconceptions about what outsourcing can and cannot do for an organization. Most have a root cause lying in an almost ideological belief that outsourcing IT is a relatively simple transaction that can more or less easily be handed over to a supplier, and that, with due monitoring, inherent benefits will follow.

But outsourcing IT is neither simple nor a transaction – it is a strategy for managing the delivery of IT services. Like all management strategies, the key lies in how the strategy is planned, implemented and managed to move the organization from its current state to its visioned future state. Outsourcing is a transition path towards that vision, not the end state. In its capacity as a management strategy, outsourcing is purely one of many strategies that may get the organization to its desired goals.

Gathering acumen is about the organization becoming an informed outsourcing purchaser and manager. Not with hindsight, as so many organizations have done, but with foresight. In this building block, the primary goal is to replace ideological concepts with realistic goals appropriate to the circumstances of the organization, its industry, and the IT markets in which it may procure services.

1.1 Discard the myths . . .

It is very important not to believe everything one is told about outsourcing IT. In particular, it is essential to do your own analysis based on your own rationale for outsourcing and the particular circumstances and potential suppliers that you will deal with. In particular, analyse supplier claims closely. In surveys we carried out in the 1993–2002 period, the most regular top sources of disappointment were hidden costs, followed by too much trust in espoused vendor claims. Unfortunately, the truth is that suppliers still tend to be much better at selling their services than customers are at buying them.

Consider the following myths as just some frequently observed examples. We are not saying here that these claims are necessarily untrue in certain circumstances. What we are saying is that they do not provide a safe general set of assumptions from which to make outsourcing decisions. Remember the words of one senior manager in a supplier company: 'Outsourcing contracts are agreed in concept but delivered in detail, and that's why they can break down.' The message – don't discount the promises; but analyse them very carefully indeed, and take real steps to secure the outcomes you really need, which may be different from the ones on offer.

Myth 1 – 'Outsourcing IT is much like outsourcing anything else (e.g. premises security, catering, rubbish disposal).'

The first point to emphasize here is that IT assets and activities take many different forms. Not all IT is the same. Do not treat IT as monolithic. A portfolio approach to managing IT needs to be taken. We categorize IT into critical differentiators, critical commodities and useful commodities. A 'critical differentiator', for example British Airways (BA) reservation system, should be kept in-house, although external resources can be bought in where necessary but will perform under internal management control. A 'critical commodity', for example aircraft maintenance systems at BA, gives no competitive advantage, but are a minimum requirement to compete in the airlines sector. These can be outsourced where supplier price and quality of performance compare favourably with the in-house option. 'Useful commodities' – data-centres, maintenance and support, payroll, accounting administration are often defined as such – are the most obvious targets for outsourcing.

However, even useful commodities cannot be compared to other resources and activities in terms of ease of outsourcing. In particular, we would point to five distinctive characteristics of IT that make it more difficult to outsource than, say, catering or advertising:

1 IT is not a homogeneous function, but comprises a wide variety of IT activities.
2 IT capabilities continue to evolve at a dizzying pace; thus predicting IT needs beyond a three-year horizon is wrought with uncertainty.
3 There is no simple basis for gauging the economics of IT activity.
4 Economic efficiency has more to do with IT practices than inherent economies of scale (see below).
5 Most distinctively of all, large switching costs are associated with IT outsourcing decisions.

When one adds that IT is increasingly entering into the core of organizational functioning, creating connectivity issues and business knock-on effects for any IT action, it also becomes clear that management of IT outsourcing takes on another characteristic, namely it is invariably going to be a learning experience, where managers need to be highly anticipatory, but will also often find themselves in catch-up mode.

Myth 2 – 'Vendors have inherent advantages in superior management practices and economies of scale. Therefore they will achieve lower IT costs while improving service.'

Case Study: a food and drinks company

We once witnessed an unsolicited bid to a food and drinks conglomerate anxious to outsource its data-centres. The supplier's representative claimed that his firm could maintain service levels and achieve 20% savings on a five-year contract, while a ten-year contract could achieve 30% cost savings. The claim was based on production and labour economies of scale, together with superior management practices inherent in a world class IT supplier. The latter arose, it was claimed, from being higher up the IT learning and experience curve than the client, superior IT management expertise not affordable by the client, and the application of best practice accumulated over many contracts. A three-hour look at the claims against the actual IT performance of the potential client revealed that it was large enough to achieve similar economies of scale itself, and that its IT management was actually very experienced. Moreover, when some of the superior management practices levels of activity by the lead supplier, do they manage other suppliers better than you can; are transaction costs really lower by going with one supplier rather than several; what are the security issues, and liabilities should something go wrong.

Myth 4 – 'Outsourcing IT is about spending as little as possible and monitoring outcomes, not managing. That can be left to the supplier.'

Organizations usually outsource IT for some mix of strategic, financial, political, technical and tactical reasons. However, the evidence is that cost savings features as one of the important expectations, and this reason always comes to the fore in recessions such as in the 1989–93 period, and also more recently throughout late 2000–03. There is plenty of evidence that cost savings can be achieved (we report on this below), but there are definite limits to suppliers working smarter to achieve the 'holy IT outsourcing trinity' of dramatic cost savings, plus a decent profit margin as well as higher service levels for the client.

In practice there will be a trade-offs between these three outcomes with, for example, significant cost savings achieved at the expense of degraded service levels, and/or lack of technology investment by the supplier. In one large-scale deal we researched in the mid-1990s, the client's senior management were satisfied with the cost savings, but operational IT had so degraded that some business units had started their own surrogate IT departments out of various budgets to counteract the poor service being received. The message: do not have unrealistic expectations about what is possible; driving hard for the cost reduction objective may well have deleterious consequences for other aspects of organizational performance. In some big deals we have seen an over-concentration on the cost objective create operational IT inflexibility and even competitive disadvantage.

However, even such a cost objective can be at risk if the client does not undertake active management on many fronts, from the pre-contract stage onwards. Practically, the client should have four major capabilities before outsourcing:

1 able to make IT sourcing decisions and formulate sourcing strategy that secures the ability of IT to leverage business performance;
2 understand the IT services market, the strategies and capabilities of individual suppliers, and what a good and bad deal looks like with a specific vendor;

3 able to articulate, negotiate and contract effectively to get what is required delivered; and

4 have in place post-contract skills and competencies that mitigate risk, elicit and deliver on business IT requirements, develop the blueprint and plans for delivery of the technology platform, and manage external supply to the organization's advantage.

In our experience the biggest omissions tend to be in area 4. This is a serious weakness because post-contract capability acts as an ultimate safety blanket for failures in establishing points 1–3. Elsewhere, we have developed a framework that suggests the need for nine core IT capabilities to fulfil this function (Feeny and Willcocks, 1998). Briefly these capabilities are:

1 IT governance and leadership.
2 Informed buying.
3 Business systems thinking.
4 Relationship building.
5 Architecture planning.
6 Technology fixing.
7 Contract facilitation.
8 Vendor development.
9 Contract monitoring.

These capabilities are discussed in full detail in the companion volume in this series (see Willcocks *et al.*, 2002). Our research shows that managing IT outsourcing successfully needs much more than a caretaker IT function consisting of an IT director and a contract monitoring function. While the new IT function will be smaller than before, it must also consist of a high performance team of individuals each with distinctive skills and competencies. Frequently new people have to be appointed to some of these roles, since the old IT function may not be a sufficient recruiting ground for the sorts of skills, orientations and abilities needed.

Our finding has been that where any of these capabilities is missing, serious problems arise. For example in two of the biggest deals globally – one a bank, the other a manufacturing company – both gave away their architecture planning function only to find the suppliers failing to develop the IT blueprint sufficiently. In one of the world's leading oil companies, relationships between client and supplier were adversarial until the client's contract manager was removed and replaced by more appropriately skilled relationship-builders and contract facilitators. In the business unit of a major manufacturing conglomerate, the IT director failed to fulfil his leadership role. Ironically, the firm had outsourced in order to give the IT function a more strategic business-focused orientation. Instead, the CIO was too busy, fire-fighting every emergency. Again, the recipe was to build up relationship-building, and contract facilitation as well as technology fixing capabilities, thus freeing up the CIO for leadership and governance. The message – on management, don't make the all-too-usual mistake of expecting too much from the supplier, and not enough from yourselves.

Myth 5 – 'Drive the hardest commercial bargain possible. The supplier will look after its own profit margin. The contract is everything.'

You may now feel very wary of suppliers. One natural instinct would be to make sure you have a watertight contract, one that the supplier cannot re-interpret or escape; one that you intend to impose to every last detail. There is also sometimes a lot of machismo in the negotiations, as well as in the operationalization of the contract. Furthermore, during 2002 we heard several advisors and commercial research organizations pointing out that IT suppliers were having a rough time, and now was the opportunity to take advantage of this and get the best cost deal possible. All this is fine, as long as you remember one thing – allow, and ensure, that the vendor makes a reasonable profit. The truth is that slim or no profit margins drives a supplier to opportunistic behaviour, can harm the relationship, and ultimately the business value of your IT performance.

Be clear that poor or onerous contracts can severely damage client–supplier relationships. Likewise lack of flexibility and common sense, or poor timing in the use of onerous contract terms. The contract is a clear fail-safe device, there to be used, but you will find that in practice it cannot predict and cover every eventuality and that active management and relationships on both sides are what lubricate effective outsourcing performance.

While it is almost a cliché to talk of win–win deals, be sure not to sign win–lose ones. In their article on 'The Winner's Curse in IT Outsourcing', Kern *et al.* (2002b) show the consequences when a supplier wins an outsourcing bid from which ultimately it stands to make no money. How does a supplier make such a mistake? Sometimes it may be a straightforward matter of miscalculation. Sometimes the in-house IT costs which the supplier has to bid against are in fact grossly, though unintentionally understated by the client. In one major deal in 2000, we found such costs understated by 50% – fortunately this was discovered during the due diligence period, otherwise the supplier would have been contractually committed to making a large loss each year for five years.

Sometimes the supplier is desperate for business and will undercut all other competitive bids, in the hope that once the work is secured the money can be recovered by additional services, and re-interpretations, or exploitation, of loopholes and ambiguities in, the contract. Whatever the cause, the effects of the winner's curse for a supplier, but also its client, can be devastating. Kern *et al.* (2002b) studied 85 completed contracts and found, amongst other things, two disturbing facts. Firstly, the winner's curse existed in nearly 20% of the cases studied (i.e. it is a much more common phenomenon than one would actually credit). Secondly, in over 75% of those cases the winner's curse was also visited on the client. In other words, if the supplier is having a bad outsourcing experience it is highly probable that this will roll on into negative repercussions for its client too.

Myth 6 – 'Outsource your IT problems. The market is now mature enough to provide superior capability to handle them.'

Contrary to this claim, we would offer a different, risk-mitigating rule of thumb: don't outsource problems. Only outsource tasks you can write a detailed specification for and can effectively monitor performance on. What is the thinking here? Surely, it is when you lack capability that the market most comes into its own. Well, yes and no. It depends on the nature of the task. In situations where the technology is well understood and stable, the precise objective can be delineated and a detailed specification can be given, it becomes relatively safe to throw the task over the wall to the IT specialists whether they be in-house or external suppliers. Not surprisingly, therefore, the most popular IT tasks that are outsourced are infrastructure and operational activities, followed by maintenance and support.

The problems occur in conditions of low technology maturity, a term coined by Feeny (1997). Technology maturity is low when either it is a new unstable technology whose business use is ill-defined, or where it is a radical new use of an existing technology, or where IT expertise with the technology is lacking.

In these cases, throwing the task over the wall to specialists needs to be replaced by a multi-functional team way of working, embracing relevant business users, managers, internal IT specialists, project managers and the buying in of external resources where necessary to work under internal management direction.

Moreover, the closer IT comes to the business and to strategy, the less advisable it is to outsource the related tasks. Development is an interesting test case here. While many organizations have outsourced development tasks, many have not, and many have also brought aspects of development capability back in-house after a period of outsourcing. This is because development involved working closely with the business and because having some capability here secured control over IT destiny and an understanding of the area, which would otherwise be abandoned to the supplier, in favour of whom asymmetries of power might develop.

A further point here is that the core IT capabilities outlined above should never really be outsourced. They provide the essential problem-solving capability that external resources, with the best will in the world, cannot supply in a sustainable way. Take 'technology fixing' for example. Outsourcing suppliers may well be able to provide routine solutions to routine problems, but it will take in-house capability to handle the non-routine technical issues that inevitably arise and for which knowledge of the business, high skills, a thorough understanding of the organization's idiosyncratic IT systems, and the ways in which they connect, are needed. Take vendor development. We have invariably found this capability developing three or four years into the contract because of what we term 'mid-contract sag' and lack of innovation. Rarely have we found new ways of leveraging the relationship emerging from a supplier's initiative. A similar case can be made for each of the other seven core IT capabilities.

Myth 7 – 'Client and supplier buying shares in each other secures superior partnering, technical innovation, risk sharing and greater business leverage.'

This approach proved quite popular in the 1990s. Examples included Delta Airlines' $US2.8 billion, 10-year agreement with AT&T, Perot Systems and Swiss Bank's 25-year $US6.2 billion deal, the 1996 Telstra–ISSC (later IBM Global Services–IBM GSA) deal with Telstra taking a 26% stake in the latter, and Lend

Lease taking a 35% stake in ISSC in exchange for a total outsourcing arrangement. We have been involved in or studied most of such deals and have to report that the advantages touted above rarely came through in any sustainable way.

A more frequent finding was that taking equity shares in a supplier or in each other often led to complacency that could also translate into indifferent service at the operational level. To be blunt, the motivational aspects of risk sharing over share ownership failed to translate to lower levels of the organization. Moreover, when complaints were made about poor service the supplier could justifiably argue that it was devoting its efforts to securing further revenues with other clients, which was also to the advantage of the present client since it owned a substantial part of the supplier! Interestingly, the Telstra deal came apart in the late 1990s and by 2002 Telstra had some five outsourcing contracts with vendors, only one of which was IBM GSA, and Lend Lease terminated the outsourcing contract while retaining equity in IBM GSA. The Perot–Swiss Bank deal came to be negotiated down to a much shorter, selective outsourcing deal, while the equity share holding arrangement was cancelled after 2000.

Myth 8 – 'Anything is going to be better than our present IT department.'

It is true that IT outsourcing can be used successfully as a catalyst for improving IT performance and galvanizing an otherwise sleepy and complacent in-house IT department. Indeed, the authors have participated in such change agentry themselves. But too many times we have also seen 'the grass is greener elsewhere' syndrome operating in favour of IT out-sourcing. Often we see in-house IT itself painted as a cash sink, a black hole into which increasing expenditure disappears with little business value merging. IT successes, or when IT is running effectively is rarely noticed, let alone praised, while IT failures, or mishaps are often very visible, and in the connected organization can have large-scale, deleterious impacts. Histor-ically, moreover, IT departments have rarely been good at internal marketing.

All this plays into the hands of the superior marketing of suppliers, who come with no perceived bad track record to the potential client's site. Against the 'IT productivity paradox' scenario of the in-house IT performance (large outlays, dis-appointing performance), the supplier can play the card of world-class supplier and of lower cost and premium service, 'superstar' performance. However, the truth of feasible performance usually lies between these two scenarios. That is you can get low cost, but also possibly degraded service, or if you want superior service from some aspects of IT you will have to pay premium prices for it. In other words, as in so many other things, in IT you will probably get what you pay for, though of course developments such as wider use of offshore outsourcing can change the equation somewhat, especially as it relates to labour costs.

The outsourcing experience may also change people's minds about the previous performance of the IT function. Frequently we have heard people complain of things like 'getting charged for everything now', of lack of flexibility in what IT can be provided, of the degree of bureaucracy and time delays involved in securing resources from the IT supplier, of lack of new, better trained supplier staff, of overall higher costs, of the constant fight for service and attention. While these are by no means the only experiences of outsourcing we could report on, where they do occur they do concentrate people's minds somewhat on whether the problems are endemic to IT rather than just to a specific service provider. Or that what happens with outsourcing is we may just change one category or set of problems for another.

A further point here is that actually, as we indicated above, you can never really outsource all of your IT department, or if you do the risks from doing so are highly prohibitive. Furthermore, to this day, a predominant majority of organizations still keep most of their IT expenditure in-house rather than with suppliers. And in fact over the last seven years, in general, we have found in-house IT functions improving in their performance relative to what the IT services market can offer. A galvanizing factor here may well have been the rising threat from IT outsourcing, which has also established a more visible benchmark for what the in-house IT function should be attaining.

The signs have been that in-house functions have been getting their houses in order much more readily in the last seven years, and indeed a supplier bid may well be (and we have seen it) used to indicate areas in which the in-house group may readily embark on a programme of self-improvement. As a final point, following on from Myth 6, it may well be that no matter how bad the IT function may be perceived to be, it still needs to be involved and needs the opportunity to improve in certain areas of IT activities. Ultimately, of course we are suggesting that to outsource properly, you need a high performance IT function in place to keep control of your IT destiny, even though this IT function will be of a very different kind from the one that went before.

1.2 Determine benefits expectations

Because ITO has been established to be a highly imitative behaviour (Loh and Venkatraman, 1992) whereby organizations attempt to duplicate the imperfectly observed success of others, there is a real need to discard the sort of myths or simplistic understandings discussed above. The need, then, is to gather acumen about the acclaimed benefits such that the organization can strategically target the use of outsourcing in a manner focused on the unique goals and characteristics of the organization. Outsourcing receives a great amount of attention spawned, in part, by the highly publicised announcements of organizations that have decided to transfer substantial parts of their IT infrastructure to external parties.

Two interesting things about these announcements. Firstly, invariably the deals are described as successes and the litany of advantages are espoused and recorded even before the supplier begins operationalizing the contract, and often before the due diligence process – which can itself change the balance of benefits – has run its course. As we know, what is expected and what gets delivered over a five- or ten-year contract can be two very different things. Secondly, there is a strong correlation observed by several studies, including our own, between announcements of large-scale outsourcing and positive improvements in the client's share price over the first ten months of a contract. This can be one reason for making such announcements of course, but the point is that this is a share market reaction, and has no real correlation to actual subsequent outsourcing performance. Those managing for the short term may well take comfort from this effect; those involved in managing, and experiencing the results of, outsourcing may be less impressed.

Despite the apparent popularity of IT outsourcing, evidence of the determinants and realized benefits are only available in accounts of individual experiences. Fortunately we have studied these over many years and can report on the real evidence. Outsourcing is often over-simplified and emotive, based on the strength of individual beliefs in its benefits or drawbacks. The most controversial aspect of outsourcing is the degree to which the espoused benefits and disadvantages are real. Yet it is important to establish real expectations about what is possible from outsourcing.

Those organizations that have outsourced IT have reported substantial benefits in a number of areas since Cullen's and Willcocks' separate and combined studies began in 1994. Figure 1.1 shows the results of Cullen's studies highlighted where substantial benefits have been achieved over three survey periods. Of particular note has been the subdued record on cost savings so often peddled as a reason to outsource. For example, in their survey of the USA and Europe, Lacity and Willcocks (2000) found only 16% reporting significant cost reduction from outsourcing IT, while only another 37% reported 'some' cost reduction. Between 30–40% also reported 'severe/difficult' problems in one or more of the strategic, cost, operational, managerial, contractual/legal and technical areas.

That said, and even with the inability of most organizations to achieve considerable cost savings from outsourcing, our studies have shown that organizations, by and large, achieve what they had chiefly set out to by outsourcing, whatever those aims were

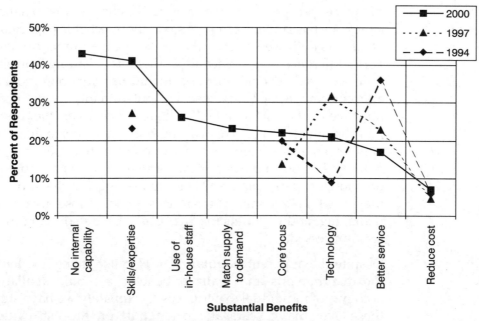

Source: Cullen et al (2001) 227-233 respondents per activity

Figure 1.1 Substantial benefits reported from outsourcing (1994, 1997, 2000)

(see Figure 1.2). This achievement has been independent of industry, company size and degree of the IT budget outsourced. Lacity and Willcocks (2000) also found the main benefits, each reported by between 33% and 44% of respondents, as being: refocus in-house IT staff, improved IT flexibility, better quality service, improved use of IT resources, and access to scarce IT/ e-business skills. Some 56% of organizations rated supplier performance as 'good' or better. Figure 1.2 also shows the results of Cullen's studies where a substantial body of organizations were achieving their primary objectives for outsourcing.

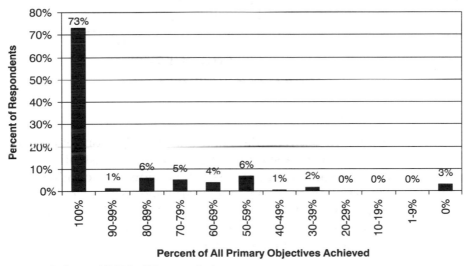

Source: Cullen et al (2001), 186 respondents

Figure 1.2 Percentage of primary objectives achieved from outsourcing

Irrespective of achieving these objectives, however, most organizations believe that ultimate success has only been moderate; likewise the degree of failure has been moderate as well (see Figure 1.3). Rarely is outsourcing seen as a total success or total failure. In their study, Lacity and Willcocks (2000) found a noticeable gap between anticipated and actual benefits. In most cases organizations were getting benefits, but invariably less than they had expected.

It is during this building block that potential benefits and goals of a potential outsourcing initiative are ascertained, along with the key lifecycle activities that will be necessary to ensure they occur. None of the above outcomes are inevitable. Management can make a real difference. For example, in an earlier study of organizations seeking primarily cost reduction we found the cost

envision that a potential deal will be done foremost on price. Although suppliers share similar characteristics, predominately centred on the profit motive, they rarely have the same approach to their customers, contracts and relationships. Even though ITO contracts tend to be shorter (three years or less – Cullen *et al.* 2001), they often have renewal terms that make the relationship much longer and the potential nature of a relationship is worth investigating at an early stage.

Table 1.1 categorizes the suppliers of outsourcing essentially into five originating types, although many are hybrids.

In practice most will try to position themselves across as many market segments as possible. In 2002 one could observe, for example, the race to become business process outsourcers amongst many of the top 30 providers. There has been much flux in recent years with the merger of IBM Global Services and PricewaterhouseCoopers consulting arm being only the

Table 1.1 Evolution of IT suppliers

Type	Description
1 *Evolved bureaux*	These suppliers evolved from data processing and time-sharing bureaux. Some of these have been in the industry more than 25 years and have grown into large multi-national outsourcing contractors
2 *IT hardware suppliers*	Moving increasingly into services as the value added opportunities from hardware sales decline. For them, outsourcing is an attempt to expand their product range, in lieu of the falling margins on hardware sales
3 *Commercialized in-house departments*	Simply selling excess capacity or becoming commercial providers. The public sector in Australia is witnessing a strong increase in these providers as government agencies are becoming commercialized and/or privatized resulting in the creation of IT service profit centres
4 *Professional services consultants*	IT service branches of consultants and system implementers who are leveraging their existing market profile as wide ranging service providers. They are increasingly offering themselves as prime contractors and subcontracting asset intensive services, like data processing, to others
5 *Niche service players*	Specialists in certain industries, services, technology, applications, etc, that are attempting to leverage their specialist capabilities

more recent example of changing strategies, new customer propositions, and attempts to spread risk and become more competitive.

Furthermore, supplier organizations tend to vary geographically. The structure, culture and services of a supplier in the US can be very different from the one in the UK and Asia Pacific, and it is worth investigating how the geographic variances may affect preliminary sourcing concepts. Global organizations that have allowed their various geographies to select their own IT suppliers often do not choose the same suppliers as their international counterparts due to local optimum value for money assessments varying with the local capabilities and prices of the suppliers. Global supplier organizations themselves often vary in their geographical capabilities and orientations.

The type of general information of most use at this formative stage of the organization's strategies is often:

- Market share in industry segments and service segments – is there local competence in the organization's industry and architecture?
- Number of customers and percent of revenue major customers represent – is there an over-reliance on a single customer?
- Financial viability – is the supplier's local business established and sustainable?
- Data-centres, solution centres, centres of excellence, etc – is there appropriate infrastructure in the locations that may service the organization's geographies?
- Use of subcontractor organizations – how do the suppliers use one another to fill capability shortfalls?
- Composition of top management – who are they and what are their backgrounds?
- Strategies – where is their focus short- and long-term, and what are their target customers, industry and services?
- Timing – are there other organizations seeking to have the supplier respond to a competitive (or non-competitive) process during the time in which the organization is considering going to market? Might there be major changes to the supplier in the foreseeable future? What impact may this have?
- If they have made low price bids in the past, find out in detail how they can do so and still make a respectable profit.

This type of information can be collected informally via discussions or more formally via a request for information process, whereby suppliers are invited to supply the required information in a formal response.

A useful assessment at this stage is to gather indicative price ranges as well. However, this is not an easy task and one that suppliers can be reluctant to contribute to without a specification process taking place first. The most common approaches are to harness the market intelligence of the organization's IT staff, if they have such knowledge, or to use consultants with sufficient commercial experience in ITO.

1.4 Conduct the comparative assessment

Many organizations have found it useful to examine their peers in terms of the sourcing strategies they have evaluated and adopted, particularly if outsourcing on the scale potentially envisaged is unfamiliar to the organization. Of course, in highly competitive industries, management may not feel free to discuss such strategies, thus organizations with similar IT architectures and scale must be sought instead. Nonetheless, a high-level industry review can often be conducted via publicly available information, but the particularly useful insight and learning is likely to be missing from such data.

As we have stated earlier, it is rare that an organization would conduct an outsourcing initiative in the same manner as it had previously, but the experience gained in the last round will be invaluable not just to the organization itself, but also to others contemplating outsourcing. The goal of this appraisal is to gather intelligence from those who have preceded the organization in sourcing strategy analysis and determine the potential implications for the organization. It is wise to cast your net wide across diverse sources when gathering knowledge. It is amazing some of the deals and suppliers we have seen customers get locked into unnecessarily when they decide to go cheap, quick and with limited scanning.

From this, the organization can obtain an indication of:

- where there are competitive markets;
- the quality of the suppliers;
- the nature of services insourced and outsourced;
- the nature of services under consideration for further outsourcing or backsourcing;

- the drivers for the decisions made;
- the structure of the deals;
- the retained organization and contract management to be put in place; and most importantly,
- the rationale, results and gained hindsight of the approaches taken.

Much of the information contained within this assessment can be gained through published reports, guides and other documents; however, we also recommend contacting key personnel at the organizations identified along with their outsourcing suppliers to gather their insights and opinions. Information from IT experts can also be made quickly available, and these may well be within the industry, ex-supplier staff, academics and from specialist consulting firms.

2

The second building block – get equipped: prepare the strategies

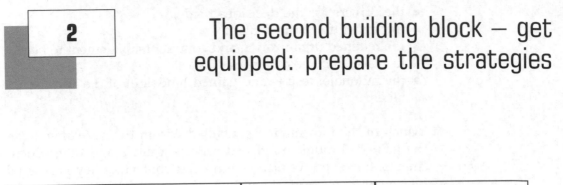

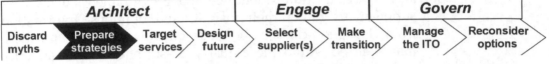

This building block, that of preparing the strategies, is crucial to the effective navigation of the entire outsourcing lifecycle. It sets the vision regarding the use of ITO within the organization along with overarching strategic preferences. Furthermore, it sets up ITO as a programme with particular emphasis on identifying the right skills at the right time and developing the communications framework. Strategy sets the parameters for what subsequently will happen. It is important to get this right. Wrong strategies create pathway inflexibilities that will be difficult and expensive to move from.

2.1 High-level sourcing decision models

Before delving into the detailed assessment of services that are strong candidates for outsourcing (Building Block 3 – 'Identify the right activities: target the services'), it is important to acknowledge the different outsourcing models and choose the right mix of models to deliver on the strategic goals the organization seeks through outsourcing. There are many forms of outsourcing and many ways to employ it strategically as a management tool.

Fundamental strategic flaws in the organization cannot be sold off – they must be understood and addressed. Applying an outsourced IT organization to an extant, flawed business model can at best only result in a more efficient version of that flawed model. Management must be able to provide the answers to these questions: where are we now, where do we want to be, and how do we get there? Outsourcing is then a management tool that can be used to leverage the resulting answers. But without such an analysis, and without integrating the outsourcing strategy with business strategy, outsourcing becomes at best a tactical device for achieving lower-level goals.

Below we present three high-level decision making frameworks that have been successfully employed by numerous organizations to determine the nature of the services best retained and those that should be investigated for outsourcing. Our objective here is to provide a tool-kit for making high-level strategic sourcing decisions. The three are:

1 MCA model – provides a framework for the organization to consider its competence relative to its peers, the maturity of the market providing the services, and the degree to which activities are core/non-core.
2 Decision tree – provides a process of elimination for options other than outsourcing to consider.
3 Modes of outsourcing – provides a framework to consider twelve different methods of outsourcing.

2.1.1 MCA (Market, Competence and Advantage) model

The prevailing view is that an organization can let go of commodity functions, but must not let suppliers get their hands on strategic areas. Others call that nonsense, use third parties where possible, just do it smart. The spiral arguments result from generalizations inappropriate on either side.

Outsourcing any part of an organization fundamentally implies an in-depth understanding of the core competencies on which the organization intends to build its future competitive advantage. Outsourcing segments of the IT infrastructure implies an in-depth understanding of what IT means to the organization and how it intends to use IT to build its competitive advantage.

One 'helicopter' model that is useful at a high level is one we have developed and used for a decade, called the MCA Model (see Figure 2.1). In this model, three dimensions are considered:

1 The **maturity** of the suppliers and the market in the relevant geographies – does the IT activity have a sustainable competitive market? How mature is it?

2 The organization's relative **competence** in the service area – how good is the organization at the services relative to competitors, other organizations, and the market in general in terms of effectiveness, cost and value? Is the organization world-class or a market leader in this activity?

3 The importance of the service in terms of its contribution to the organization's sustainable **competitive advantage** – what IT-related activity is critical to build and sustain competitive advantage now and in the future? Is it the outcome of that activity that creates the advantage (output) or the process of doing the activity (experience)?

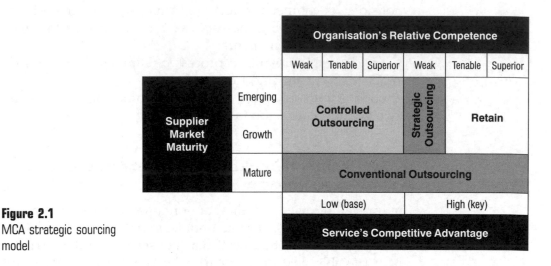

Figure 2.1
MCA strategic sourcing model

If you look at, and use, Figure 2.1, you will see that your analysis needs to do three things:

1 Look at the maturity of the market.

If the market is mature with many suppliers, can the organization exploit it to achieve significant business leverage? Is the organization vertically integrated for historical rather than strategic reasons? If the market is mature, a conventional outsourcing arrangement can be the starting point.

If the market is immature (few suppliers or immature capabilities), a greater degree of control is required to ensure ongoing benefits, accelerate the market's capabilities, and have alternative competitive supply; hence a more controlled style of outsourcing is required. Control can be obtained through numerous means – for example, split portfolio outsourcing (use of more than one supplier), joint ventures, outsourcing one part, and packaging further parts for competitive bid at a later stage, but offering the incumbent supplier the first bid for this subsequent work. Another alternative, if you are more competent in an IT activity in terms of cost and capability than the market, is to keep this in-house for the meantime, and look to outsource later when the market has caught up on performance.

2 Look at the organization's relative competence.

Are there activities that can deliver competitive advantage, but the organization does not possess the competence? Strategic sourcing can bring that competence to the organization, but it will need to design the arrangement to transfer the requisite knowledge while keeping its options open for in-house sourcing as its relative competence grows. If the competence is a key contributor to competitive advantage we recommend that the market be used on a 'buy-in' or 'insource' basis – that is placing those external resources under active in-house management control.

Does the organization have at least a tenable position in competitive advantage activities where the market is not mature? The organization will want to retain these services in-house and not let its competitors have access via suppliers. It may also choose to buy in external competencies to work under in-house management control, and facilitate transfer of learning in order to build the competence further. However, some organizations use this superiority to offer value to other organizations through commercializing the in-house activity. We have seen this, for example, with development shops in the UK National Health Service, while Phillips Electronics over several years helped to form Origin to sell its development and operational IT capability on the IT services market.

3 Look at activities not critical for competitive advantage.

If an activity is not creating competitive advantage, is the organization overly investing in it? It still may be critical to strategic direction – witness the aircraft maintenance systems example at British Airways cited in Chapter 1, a critical commodity, but not a critical differentiator. There may be better investments an organization can make with its human/asset capital for greater effect. In fact, retaining marginal, or even critical commodity, activities may result in competitive disadvantage if competitors are leveraging scarce resources better. Being the best at non-advantage activities is easy to be proud of, but should the organization be best at something else?

If the organization is at least competent at a non-core IT activity, it may have unlocked value that can be realized through a sale of the function, then could use an outsourcing contract to provide ongoing service. The market maturity will then drive the type of outsourcing model needed – whether it is controlled or conventional.

2.1.2 Decision tree

This decision tree starts out with a fresh look at what the organization is doing with high-level re-engineering. It then offers alternatives such as:

- Discontinuing the services altogether, if no longer required.
- Outsourcing if the organization itself does not need to perform the services, but instead can be more effective by purchasing the outputs.

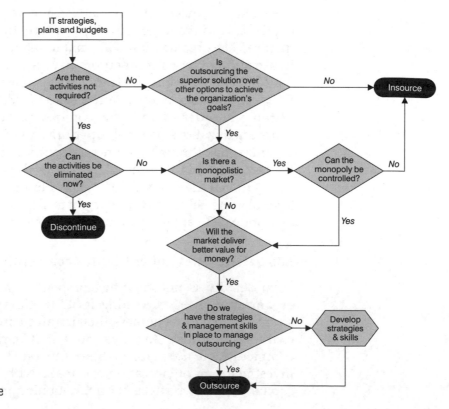

Figure 2.2
Sourcing decision tree

Table 2.1 Sourcing decision tree question process

Question	Decision process
Are there activities not required in the future?	If an activity will not be required in the future, the organization should begin the removal process. Outsourcing has been used as a 'ramp-down' mechanism where the goal is to purchase ever-decreasing outputs until the organization has no need for further services. Be aware, however, that more often than not, the need has continued far beyond the projected exit date
Can the organization be more effective performing the activity or using the output?	If the organization needs to perform the activities itself because of the superior benefits the conduct of the process offers, rather than the smart use of the outputs, consider keeping the activity in-house and having performance improvement initiatives
Is there potential for a monopolist supplier market?	There are two key drivers of a potential monopoly: (1) a lack of a competitive market and (2) the degree of organizational specificity involved. A competitive market is a key requirement to ensure the organization is not held to ransom by a monopolist supplier. It also allows for more outsourcing options including the use panels and multiple suppliers for the best-of-breed approach. Specificity allows an organization to be potentially 'held to ransom' if any of the following are present: ● Site specificity – location of the services limits the range of available suppliers. ● Technical specificity – assets to be employed are very specific to the organization (hardware, software, etc) ● Human specificity – where the service delivery individuals must develop in-depth skills unique to the organization
Can the organization control the monopolist characteristics of the potential supplier market?	There may be such benefits in moving services to an external party that the organization may be willing to enter into a known potential monopolistic supply situation. Not all ITO has had a mature market prior to an organization outsourcing and it has been successful. However, the control of a potential monopoly requires strong risk management techniques
Will the market deliver better value for money?	At the end of the day, the supplier will need to make the required profit and the organization must have a better total cost structure. Determining the total cost under either the insource or outsource option is one to which much diligence should be applied, as cost saving under either approach is often touted in theory and elusive in practice
Does the organization have the strategies and management skills in place?	If the organization is not ready to manage the outsourcing solution, it must take the time to get ready. On the job, trial and error methods are rarely the most cost-effective manner to get the results outsourcing was designed to achieve. The lack of ability should not prevent outsourcing, only becomes an early, critical emphasis

- Internal performance improvement if the organization must perform the services itself or cannot obtain value for money from a competitive market.

The outsourcing decision tree provides a tool for logically thinking through the decision process (see Figure 2.2). It begins by taking into account the future strategies, plans and budgets for IT within the organization, as does any outsourcing strategy. It then leads the decision-makers through a process to determine the responses to the questions in Table 2.1.

The following real life case study illustrates what happens when this sort of detailed analysis is short-circuited.

Case Study: a law enforcement agency

The IT helpdesk of the agency was outsourced to a contract labour organization in an attempt to improve user satisfaction and promote new professional ways of working. However, unbeknownst to management at the time, the nature of the calls to the helpdesk were very specific to the organization and required detailed knowledge, not only of the systems, but of the process of law enforcement. It took about six months to get the helpdesk fully operational and then the officers were redeployed and the labour firm took over full operations. The agency signed a one-year agreement, as it wanted to be able to competitively tender frequently to ensure low cost service delivery. During the next round of tendering, the agency discovered it had created a monopoly due to the very specific nature of the knowledge the incumbent supplier now had. No bid came close to the incumbent supplier, that had doubled its price in the tender.

2.1.3 Modes of outsourcing

In earlier work, we have pointed to the plethora of sourcing options now available. It is useful at this point to spell out the major ones, and make some comment on their track record. Be aware that while some practices have better track records than others, much depends on the quality of risk mitigation and management practices put in place to run them. We discussed the relative advantages and issues in selective versus total outsourcing in Chapter 1. The main finding is worth reiterating: that selective outsourcing tends to be the lower risk option, while total outsourcing (80% or more of the IT budget with the market) is really best done by an organization that has matured its ability to manage large-scale outsourcing. Twelve options are now discussed that can be used selectively, or as part of a total outsourcing deal:

1 *Transitional outsourcing* – handing over legacy systems to enable in-house focus on building the new IT world. Generally an effective, low risk use of the market.

2 *Value-added outsourcing* – combining client and vendor strengths in order to market IT products or services commercially. Nice, logical idea, but in practice such components of a larger IT outsourcing deal have been too small too attract priority attention. Moreover, implementation looks a lot less attractive when it is realized that it requires nine times the initial development costs to commercialize a product/service, and there are no guaranteed paybacks in a competitive market.

3 *Equity holdings* – has a mixed record, as discussed in Chapter 1.

4 *'Co-sourcing'* – a term coined by EDS whereby the supplier takes over an activity, or works with a client on it, and gets paid for improvements in the client's business results. Again a mixed record because many factors can affect supplier performance that may well be out of its control; also, suppliers' cultures have not always been set up to work in this way.

5 *Multiple suppliers* – the preferred option by most client organizations. It follows a 'horses for courses', 'best-of-breed' logic and spreads risk. At the same time there are additional transaction and management cost incurred by taking the multiple supplier route. Probably needs each supplier to be managed individually, as companies like BP Exploration and Dupont have not always found suppliers managing each other the most productive arrangement.

6 *Spin-offs* – creating a separate company out of an effective IT function, and allowing it to sell its services on the open market, as well as back to the original host company. EDS grew out of General Motors in this way. With a Dutch software house, Philips created Origin that proved fairly successful during the 1990s. The general record is not a good one, however. It takes a lot of new marketing,

customer-focused and financial skills to commercialize an IT department, and the market is very competitive indeed for those with no previous track record.

7 *Application service provision/'netsourcing'* – renting applications, services and infrastructure over networks. Web services are the potential means to an expansion in this market, although its development was put on hold during the recession beginning in late 2000. Our own study (Kern *et al.* 2002a) demonstrates that the model has compelling logic. Once the technology is sorted out, and suppliers can find a winning business model that will attract customers on an upswing in the economy, or can find ways of cutting customer costs dramatically and reliably, we anticipate this is a real one to watch for the medium-term future.

8 *Business process outsourcing* – in cost-pressured economies, a fast-growing market in 2002/3 because of the latent cost reductions inherent in streamlining indifferently managed back-offices and business processes and applying IT to the result. However, the market is still developing, with some good niche players and start-ups, but no one supplier yet looks able to service all a customer's business process needs. Beware of supplier claims here, since many have been all too quick to jump into a potential growth area in an otherwise weak IT climate. Check that the marketing is matched by capabilities.

9 *Backsourcing* – bringing aspects of IT back in-house after originally outsourcing them. Thus Lend Lease Corporation brought back aspects of systems development several years into a long-term deal with IBM Global Services. East Midlands Electricity actually cancelled its 1992 12-year deal with Perot Systems in 1999, taking advantage of a clause permitting cancellation in the event of a merger (it merged with Powergen that year). From 1995 it had redefined the importance of IT to the business and began re-building its in-house skills. More often there is a steady creep back, as a result of changing requirements and contexts, or from a realization that the activity was in fact better positioned in-house all along.

10 *Shared services* – for example in accounting services or e-procurement exchanges. Here, several customers identify a non-competitive area worth outsourcing together to the same supplier. Thus, seven oil companies outsourced accounting administration to Accenture, based in Aberdeen, Scotland. The aim here is to achieve significant cost reductions through economies of scale.

11 *Offshore outsourcing* sometimes billed as 'cheaper, quicker, better', suppliers in this market have been moving aggressively, with India cornering over 80% of the revenues by 2002, but with Russia and China, amongst others, beginning to position themselves to take more of the market. Initially focused on programming and low-level technical activity in which offshore economies had a significant labour cost advantage, the bigger players show an ability to move up the IT value chain quickly, including developing high quality technical skills bases. Management and transaction costs can be higher with this form of outsourcing, however. Some companies have already established 'nearshore' operations in customer countries, while some IT suppliers and customers have themselves established facilities in developing economies. Definitely one to watch and think about.

12 *Joint venture* – client and supplier establishing a third entity through which to resource and share risks and rewards. As one example, FI Group and the Royal Bank of Scotland established the jointly owned First Banking Systems in 1999. It was given a budget of £150 million over five years to develop commercial software and manage IT planning and architecture. It was actually terminated in 2002. In 2001/2 in the business process outsourcing market Xchanging took a modified model and created four enterprises with three clients to commercialize their back offices. Our own studies of these show an effective set of results over the first two years of operation (Feeny *et al.* 2003).

2.2 Determine the organization's strategic preferences

There are many decisions to be made when designing outsourcing strategies, for which most organizations would benefit by having a preferred corporate approach that has been determined at the appropriate level in the organization. Frequently, however, outsourcing projects are delegated to mid-level management, and where some level of corporate guidance on a few key strategic issues is lacking, decisions run the danger of being made without the holistic view required.

These corporate preferences should typically include, but are not limited to guidance on:

1 Criteria to apply in identifying outsourcing candidates.
2 Use of in-house bids.
3 Multiple vs. limited number of suppliers.

4 Staff transfer approaches.
5 Asset ownership.
6 Intellectual property.
7 Governing documents employed.
8 Risk/reward program.
9 Risk management.
10 Short- vs. long-term contracts.

Let us look at these in more detail.

2.2.1 Criteria to apply in identifying target services

Criteria need to be set initially as part of indicating what services can potentially be targeted for outsourcing. This assists the decision-making process, particularly if such decision-making is delegated or decentralized.

Case Study: outsourcing criteria in an airline

A major airline created a working group of its dozen executives to determine outsourcing opportunities as a part of a business review process. The airline had performed outsourcing at a piecemeal tactical level, with each out-sourcing project being conducted with varying degrees of success. As its cost structures were the highest in the region, it was appropriate that it take a high-level strategic view of outsourcing across the entire company. The executives determined that outsourcing would be most advantageous where the following short- and long-term benefits could be met provided that barriers identified were not present. It created the following list:

Short-term benefits

- Existing or potential market for improved service and value for money.
- Align supply to demand where there is a backlog or unsatisfied demand.
- Substantially upgrade services without a capital investment.
- Cash infusion from the sale of assets or transfer of staff.
- Reduce cost in areas in which costs are above industry standard.
- Access to staff and skills in short supply.

Long-term benefits

- Enable a strategic focus.
- Enable a better customer focus.
- Enable positive cultural change.

Barriers

- Activity is core.
- Customer perceptions will be adverse.
- Regulatory restrictions or imperatives.
- Risk of creating a monopolistic market due to organizational specifity.
- The airline has a sustainable competitive advantage.

This list served the organization well, as previously each department head had identified other departments that could be outsourced while emphatically arguing against the outsourcing of their own departments. An objective list of criteria allowed the organization to be systematic in its identification of target services rather than relying on the persuasiveness of the individual executives.

2.2.2 Use of in-house bids

Internal bidding refers to where an internal team is a bidder alongside potential external suppliers and, if successful, supplies the required service on a commercial, contractual basis. Commonly accepted probity principles dictate that it operates with the same principles as an external bid. However, some organizations have explicitly stated that the in-house bid will be given either preference (by some weighting factor) or the opportunity to 'better' the external bids.

In-house bids should be considered with caution; they are more complicated than just adding one more bid to be evaluated. The success of the tender effort will be largely determined by external suppliers' confidence in the equality of treatment or 'level playing field'. If they doubt the integrity of the process, they will be reluctant to respond. Suppliers may interpret in-house bids as an indication that tendering is not a genuine market exercise, and it is perhaps being used for 'free benchmarking', or to learn how to improve internal operations.

2.2.3 Multiple vs. limited number of suppliers

A key decision is one of whether the organization has a strategic preference to employ minimal or multiple points of supplier accountability in its supplier portfolio. An industry norm has not emerged as to which is generally preferable; customers are evenly split between the use of both models – many suppliers or few suppliers, albeit the use of preferred suppliers is most predominate, as shown in Figure 2.3 (Cullen *et al.*, 2001).

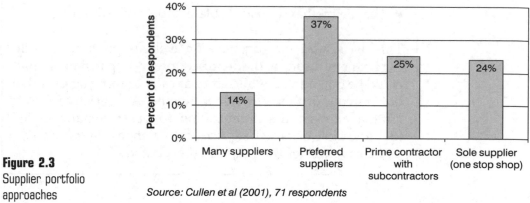

Figure 2.3
Supplier portfolio approaches

Source: Cullen et al (2001), 71 respondents

Table 2.2 Points of accountability options

Points of accountability	Methods	Potential advantages	Potential disadvantages
Few	Prime contractor with subcontractors or sole 'one-stop-shop' supplier	• Total accountability • Streamlined contact • End-to-end KPIs can be implemented	• Over-dependence on the supplier • Relationship hindrance between the organization and subcontractors • Comprise best of breed solutions
Multiple	More than one supplier performing similar/ substitutable services or a pre-qualified supplier panel from which contracts are let	• Less over-dependence risk • Continuous competitive market with ready alternate supply • Can choose best of breed suppliers • Facilitates benchmarking	• Higher management and coordination cost • KPIs only reflect individual suppliers span of control • Coordination between suppliers – act as 'satellites'

Table 2.2 rehearses the options and different levels of advantage and disadvantage. A frequent question we are asked is, in fact: what is the optimum number of suppliers? One answer is itself a question: what are you trying to achieve, in what circumstances? Another is: if you have ten you probably have too many, if you have one or two, probably too few!

2.2.4 Staff transfer approaches

There is no 'right' approach for dealing with staff that may be affected by the outsourcing arrangement. A balance must occur between the best long-term interest of the organization, the affected staff, and the supplier. The two basic strategies are shown in Table 2.3.

Regardless of the approach, best practice has the client organization providing such services as career and finance planning,

Table 2.3 Staff transfer approaches

Approach	Description	Advantages	Disadvantages
Clean Break	Staff deemed excess and subject to redundancy. Employment offers by the supplier not guaranteed	• Enables a 'clean sheet' for the supplier to determine who it wants to hire and the employment conditions • All excess staff are treated the same • Redundancy payouts may lessen negative reactions to the outsourcing initiative	• Supplier may need guaranteed transfers to provide the service and prefer to lock them • Double dipping – staff that take the supplier's offer have a similar job and a redundancy payout at the same time • High potential cost of payouts
Negotiated Transfer	Some or all staff are transferred to the supplier and the employment conditions agreed in advance	• Avoid large redundancy payouts • Can lessen disruptions to productivity during process if staff is informed of employment prospects and conditions • Shows commitment to employee welfare to the workforce as a whole	• Transmission of business rules in each governing law locality must be considered • Increased negotiations likely to be required • Higher overall price if transfers are forced – if the supplier does not want all the staff or employment conditions are onerous compared to the supplier's profitability model

outplacement and training to enable staff to have the best possible opportunity for future employment.

2.2.5 Asset ownership

Economists recommend that the party that can more efficiently invest in the asset should own it. Whoever will benefit from maximizing total productivity and increasing the value of the asset, there the ownership should reside. The general preference for most organizations that outsource is to divest to the supplier the assets required to perform the outsourced services.

An exception to this preference would be if continued ownership of the asset is required for business contingency purposes. This would be the case if such an asset were unique to the organization and not reasonably available elsewhere. Thus transferring the asset would increase the potential for the supplier to have monopolistic power. Intellectual property may also be considered an asset, and also invites careful consideration.

2.2.6 Intellectual property

Best practice to encourage innovation in suppliers is to give them appropriate intellectual property rights (IPR) with regard to the intellectual property they develop in the course of delivering services. In this way, the supplier has a higher degree of motivation as they can use the IPR in other services.

However, there may be instances in which the organization will require IPR should the contract be terminated for whatever reason. In this event, the organization needs to insist on appropriate rights to use the intellectual property and may require some form of escrow in event of termination. In the best practice contract these IPR and termination clauses will be developed in detail.

2.2.7 Governing documents employed

The governing documents comprise the key agreement documents that will be employed to preside over the arrangement. The contract is the foremost document. However, there are many alternatives to the other forms of governing documents, for example the use of a Service Level Agreement versus other forms of specifications, and various procedural 'manuals'. These are discussed in the fourth Building Block – 'Ensure the results:

design the future' Corporate standards and documentation regarding outsourcing governance will deliver consistency and accelerate any outsourcing initiative.

2.2.8 Risk/reward programme

Where possible, the better practice involves moving towards a risk/reward structure rather than a straight fee-for-service arrangement. It is preferable that the organization has a principle regarding whether to use risk (financial consequences) and/or rewards (financial bonuses) in its outsourcing arrangements. Corporate preferences can be set for the approach taken: the percent of the per annum contract value to put at risk or put towards a bonus, whether to employ consequence escalation, and other options (refer to Building Block 4 – 'Ensure the results: design the future').

Financial consequences for consistent or significant failure to meet Key Performance Indicators (KPIs) exist in the majority of ITO contracts. The amounts should be sufficient enough to motivate the supplier to avoid the consequences, but should not incapacitate the supplier (e.g. harm profit but not harm viability). From a client business perspective, proper service performance is nearly always worth more than any rebate. However, should consistent or significant failure to meet the KPIs occur, invocation of the termination clause should be an option.

A word of caution – penalties are not damages in the legal sense, thus in the event of breach they are rarely up-held. Courts award actual damages, not punitive ones. The most one can expect from successful litigation over a contract is payment of actual damages incurred.

Like risk consequences, reward 'bonuses' are used to guide suppliers' motivation and behaviour. Rewards for excelling beyond minimum expectations are desirable if the organization would benefit from this higher level of performance. Rewards are not recommended to be applied carte blanche, but rather only in areas that are important to the organization.

2.2.9 Risk management

Risk management and sound internal controls are required in any business process regardless of how sourced. Any outsourcing arrangement introduces new risks or requires organizations to manage existing risks in a different manner. Such risks include non-performance, breach, early termination, disputes, and liability issues. Every organization has certain risks that will require special attention. These include:

1 The organization does not have a core competence in outsourcing, thus large-scale outsourcing may not be prudent with regard to risk management.
2 Outsourcing must take into account the interrelation of operations and risk of disruption.
3 Information security and disaster recovery is of utmost importance to ensure service continuity and comply with privacy rules.
4 If potentially outsourced services are likely to be a comparatively large scale for the supplier market and geographically dispersed, the client needs to ensure suitable coverage of supply and large volume capacity.
5 There may be specialized assets and knowledge required for this industry and there may be only a few competitors in certain markets. This requires risk management over potentially monopolistic suppliers or building a competitive supply market.

2.2.10 Short- vs. long-term contracts

The majority of ITO contracts now have terms of three years or less (Cullen *et al.*, 2001), but are more 'roll-over' orientated, thus include options for extensions. These extensions are typically one to two years per extension. In our view, these are sensible arrangements because they contract for relatively stable periods in volatile economic and technological environments, provide flexibility for both client and supplier, while also permitting the basis of a long-term relationship. The optimum length of a contract is often driven by the:

● amortization period of the assets involved;
● amortization of transition-in costs where a separate transition-in fee has not been incorporated;
● level of competition in the market and price trends;
● ability and willingness of the organization to switch suppliers;
● the strategic planning cycle of the organization; and
● the degree of specific organizational knowledge required by the supplier, hence the investment required by the organization to instil such knowledge.

2.3 Decide the outsourcing approach

There is no one approach to outsourcing. In practice, organizations use the following approaches and, typically, in a hybrid fashion. The important issue is that the approach is determined as part of a carefully crafted strategy, rather than one that occurred haphazardly. In Table 2.4 we point to three approaches that we have seen used both effectively and ineffectively at different times over the last decade. In the diagram we summarize the major learning on the advantages and disadvantages of the three approaches, and what needs to be in place to make each effective.

2.4 Identify the outsourcing lifecycle competencies required

Outsourcing should be a strategy, and not merely reduced to a cost reduction exercise. Like all management strategies, success depends on how wisely it is planned, deployed and managed. One person can rarely conduct the outsourcing journey alone. Ideally, many different areas of expertise may be present in one individual; however, this is rare. The best results are achieved when many perspectives contribute throughout the lifecycle.

There are a number of skill sets required and many of these skills will flow from one phase to another. Only some skills may require a full time commitment. The task is to ensure that the required expertise is represented in an effective team.

The following Table 2.5 and matrix in Figure 2.4 have been designed to assist in planning the lifecycle stages and to ensure that the pertinent expertise is incorporated at the appropriate time. To give one example, on the EDS–UK Inland Revenue ten-year £1 billion deal back in 1992/3 there were over 20 people involved on the client side to get to contract, and these were spread right across the skills detailed in Table 2.5.

In Figure 2.4 we break down the activities that must be conducted across the lifecycle in an IT outsourcing deal of any size, and how these map on to the skills delineated in Table 2.5. Additionally, bear in mind that the IT function must also build up its in-house core capabilities (see Chapter 1, Myth 4), many of which can be employed on these manifold lifecycle tasks, as well as elsewhere.

Table 2.4 Outsourcing approaches

Approach	Strength	Weakness	Requirements to be effective
Big Bang *Significant portions of all activities are outsourced at one time. Reported often in the media but less used in practice*	1 More interest from suppliers due to potential revenue 2 Centralized program and lower coordination costs 3 Management more strategically involved 4 Enables organization-wide learning 5 End-to-end KPIs	1 Greater risk and impact 2 Resource intensive 3 More stakeholders 4 Can attract public attention 5 Complex and requires significant management 6 Supplier may not have all requisite skills	• The organization should re-engineer practices and work flows to make it work • Management should be more strategically involved due to the impact • The organization should be 'outsourcing ready' – it must be an expert, or get the expertise
Piecemeal *Each activity is outsourced independently over time and a variety of suppliers are used. Most common approach, but often by default rather than by design*	1 Best supplier and price obtained for each outsourced activity at the time 2 Staggers risk of disruption 3 Solve needs as they arise 4 Less complexity, thus manageable at lower levels 5 Can incorporate lessons into future deals, if knowledge is shared	1 May not be best value overall, over time 2 High coordination costs and duplication of effort 3 Synergies difficult 4 Adversity between suppliers with 'blaming' at interface points 5 Isolated lessons 6 Less able to attract major suppliers 7 Piecemeal KPIs not end-to-end	• There should be an organization-wide mechanism for sharing best practices and lessons learnt • Service interdependencies should be well understood • Completely unambiguous responsibilities should be defined between all parties • Contracts require novation options in the event that greater efficiency/effectiveness can be achieved by re-bundling or unbundling at later stages

Incremental

One or more suppliers are selected for pilot project(s) with planned escalation of outsourcing. Escalation occurs if preceding outsourcing is successful

1 Immediate needs met through pilots
2 Staged approach and evolved prototyping – the organization and supplier improve each addition
3 Supplier has incentive to 'prove' itself to obtain more work
4 Attracts interest from suppliers due to potential revenue stream

1 Longer time frame
2 Supplier likely to continuously seek escalation of outsourcing irrespective of organization's readiness
3 Maintaining momentum

- Should be managed as a continuous programme
- Organization should have clear understanding of what services will be subject to further outsourcing
- Requires commitment to further outsourcing or lose commitment from supplier(s)
- Each deal should be designed to include the lessons learnt from the previous projects
- Requires outsourcing escalation criteria

Building Block Activities	Audit	Commercial	Communication	Financial	Management	Legal	Technical	User
1 Prepare Strategies								
1.1 Strategic sourcing		✓	✓	✓	✓			
1.2 Market research		✓		✓			✓	
1.3 Industry comparative		✓					✓	
1.4 Strategic preferences		✓			✓			
1.5 Competency framework		✓		✓	✓		✓	✓
1.6 Communication		✓	✓		✓			✓
2 Target Services								
2.1 Identification		✓			✓		✓	
2.2 Service profiling		✓		✓			✓	✓
2.3 Outsourcing approach		✓		✓	✓		✓	✓
2.4 Base Case		✓		✓			✓	
2.5 Feasibility/impact		✓		✓	✓		✓	✓
3 Design Future								
3.1 Arrangement model		✓	✓	✓	✓	✓	✓	✓
3.2 Contract		✓		✓	✓	✓	✓	✓
3.3 SLA		✓		✓			✓	✓
3.4 Pricing		✓		✓	✓		✓	✓
3.5 Retained organization & arrangement management		✓	✓	✓	✓		✓	✓
3.6 Transition & transfer		✓	✓	✓		✓	✓	

Skills/Perspectives

Skills matrix (checkmarks indicate required skill for each building block activity; column headers not shown on this page):

Activity	1	2	3	4	5	6
4 Select Supplier(s)						
4.1 Selection stages	✓		✓	✓		✓
4.2 Selection strategy		✓	✓	✓		✓
4.3 Probity plan		✓				✓
4.4 Bid package		✓	✓	✓		✓
4.5 Evaluation & business case	✓	✓	✓	✓	✓	✓
4.6 Negotiation	✓	✓	✓	✓		✓
5 Make Transition						
5.1 Conduct transfer	✓	✓			✓	✓
5.2 Setup retained organization & arrangement management	✓	✓		✓		✓
5.3 Workflow re-engineering	✓	✓				✓
5.4 Procedures & protocols	✓	✓		✓		✓
6 Manage Supplier(s)						
6.1 Payment	✓	✓				✓
6.2 Variations & disputes		✓	✓	✓		✓
6.3 Reviews, evaluations & audits	✓	✓	✓	✓		✓
6.4 Planing & forecasting		✓	✓	✓		✓
6.5 Administration & recordkeeping	✓	✓	✓	✓		✓
6.6 Relationship management		✓	✓		✓	✓
6.7 Continuous improvement		✓	✓			✓
7 Reconsider Options						
7.1 Arrangement, industry & market review		✓	✓			✓
7.2 Options & bus case	✓	✓	✓	✓		✓
7.3 Implementation plan	✓	✓	✓	✓		✓

Figure 2.4 Example building block skills matrix

Table 2.5 Building block skills description

Expertise	Expertise in:
Audit	performance, financial and technical reviews, evaluations and audit techniques
Commercial	the ITO market, commercial ITO practices and techniques, ITO project management
Communication	the preparation and delivery of effective communications to the appropriate stakeholders in addition to organizational change management techniques
Financial	accounting, the organization's financial system and requirements, pricing, financial assessments, due diligence
Legal	ITO contracts
Management	organizational strategies, politics, business processes and their key interfaces with IT service delivery
Technical	industry practices and technologies and organizational operations regarding the targeted services
User	intimate knowledge of user/customer needs, expectations and business processes

2.5 Prepare the communications strategy

The word 'outsourcing' will spread like wildfire across the organization with a plethora of rumours about the organization's motives. The 'FUD' factor is created – fear, uncertainty and doubt. Be proactive, not reactive, in driving the communication. Do not let rumour drive beliefs. The one thing staff hate more than anything in times of change is uncertainty.

Any organization will need to be communicating with a variety of people over the course of the outsourcing lifecycle. The degree of communication has often come as a surprise and, time after time, has not been appropriately planned for and resourced. Communications will be a combination of the formal and informal, on a mass and individual basis. Effective communication is best provided in the manner most meaningful to the stakeholder. In Table 2.6, we indicate the typical questions that will be asked by major stakeholders in a typical outsourcing event. We then also spell out the communications options most suitable for answering these questions across the stakeholder base.

Table 2.6 Communication stakeholders

Internal stakeholder	Issues	Options
Staff	How will I be affected? What are my options? How do I explore them? What assistance will I be given? What is working for a supplier like? When is it all going to happen? What is expected of me now?	● Open forums ● Meetings ● Newsletters ● Counselling ● Email ● Hotline
Customers/users	How will this affect service? How can we ensure our needs will be met? Who should we be talking to?	● Liaison groups ● Briefings ● Newsletters
Human resources department	Which employees will be affected? Who will remain, transferred, made redundant, etc? What precedence has been set within the organization and by other organizations? What is our role?	● Meetings ● Working party ● Steering committee involvement
Finance/accounting department	What is the budget for the project? How will the supplier be paid for different services? Will there be interfaces to our financial systems? Will there be any asset sales? What is our role?	● Meetings ● Working party ● Steering committee involvement
Legal department	What sort of contract will be signed? What are the applicable laws? Will we be using external lawyers to draft the contract? What is our role?	● Meetings ● Working party ● Steering committee involvement
Management	What are all the options being considered? What are other organizations' experiences? What are our competitors doing? Who are the potential suppliers? What is the bottom line impact and what are other benefits? What risks are present and how will we manage them? What is the schedule? What are the key issues?	● Steering committee involvement ● Progress reports ● Meetings
External stakeholder	**Issues**	**Options**
Suppliers	What products/services are desired? What is the contract worth? How long is the contract? What sort of relationship is desired? Who should we be talking to? What is the timetable?	● Briefings ● Site visits ● Informal discussions
Media	Who won? How much is it worth? What will change? Will there be job losses?	● Press releases ● Interviews

It is important to develop a comprehensive communications plan. In Table 2.7 we list the main headings of such a communications plan.

While all stakeholders will require some form of communication, consider focusing the efforts on individuals and groups that are critical to success and that will take a major effort on your part to get them to buy into the organizational messages and direction. Figure 2.5 helps to target effort here. 'Woo & win' and 'maintain confidence' require giving stakeholders continuous access to information and quick resolution of their questions/issues. Use frequent face-to-face interactions and formal processes for soliciting feedback and monitoring effectiveness. For audiences less immediately critical to the outsourcing project one can use a variety of media, with less emphasis on face-to-face communication.

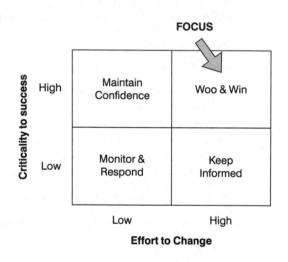

Figure 2.5
Communication focus matrix

In all this, you will find Figure 2.6 particularly useful for analysing where you are with communication, and what now needs to be done.

As can be seen, we posit three phases that stakeholders need to be moved through – from preparation, through acceptance to commitment. These break down into eight, more detailed stakeholder states. The main purpose of the communications strategy is to move all the stakeholders through the stages of differing commitment, by providing the appropriate communications at the appropriate times. The organization will need to

Table 2.7 Communication strategy components

Audience	Key messages	Purpose/objective	Vehicle	Timing	Delivery	Preparation	Feedback process
Who needs to be contacted? Where does each audience currently stand?	What concept, knowledge, appreciation needs to be communicated to each audience? Do we need to inform them or change their opinions, perceptions, or beliefs?	Why are we initiating these communications? Do we need to change their opinions, perceptions or beliefs?	How can we leverage existing communication channels? What form of communication does each audience respond to best? What is most cost effective?	When should each message be conveyed? What are our 'drop dead' dates?	Who should deliver each message? Whom does each audience trust?	Who is most appropriate to prepare the message What is the most appropriate vehicle/chosen media?	How will we track that the message is getting through? Do we want to get feedback? How will we demonstrate that we received the feedback and it is being actioned?

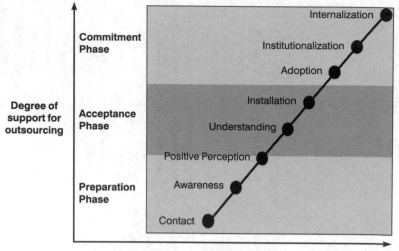

Figure 2.6

Stages of commitment to organizational change model

Phase	Description
Preparation	This phase has primarily public, one-way forms of communication (i.e. a management presentation). The big picture information about the outsourcing initiative is required.
Acceptance	The "Acceptance Phase" is then about providing time to test and walk through the change in the employee's mind - with the organization's management continually providing encouragement and information.
Commitment	This phase is the hardest one to move change targets through as it requires targets to recognise and truly support (inwardly, not outwardly) the "new way." More one-to-one communication will be needed - talking in more detail about the precise nature of how outsourcing will affect each individual, not the organization. This is where the real selling of outsourcing - its positive benefits for the individual, needs to occur.

know where it is on the graph at any moment, in order to know how to pitch its communication and strategy-selling activities.

Throughout your communication planning, of course, it is important to have the supplier also fully involved and integrated into the process. Indeed, because of the number of outsourcing deals experienced suppliers have been involved in, invariably they have invaluable insights and knowledge to bring to carrying out the communications process. Indeed, many have by now finely honed their people communication and transition strategies over many years.

3

The third building block – identify the right activities: target the services

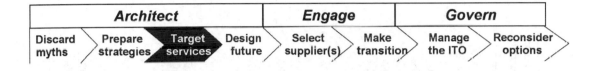

There are no hard and fast rules as to what should be outsourced and what should not. It is more appropriate to talk of levels of risk involved in taking certain courses of action, and how these can be mitigated. There is one exception here. We have already suggested that it is a bad idea to outsource 'critical differentiators', but these themselves may become commodified over time and no longer be sources of competitive advantage. As such they can then become targets for outsourcing. Certainly, some types of services are more popular targets for outsourcing, particularly those with mature markets, service predictability and well-known industry performance standards.

For example, in Australia the nature of ITO decisions has resulted in the most frequently outsourced IT activities being related to infrastructure (hardware support and WAN), applications (development and support), systems integration and education (see Table 3.1). We regularly find similar patterns in Europe and the USA. Thus Lacity and Willcocks (2001) report the main activities targeted as disaster recovery, mainframe operations, network management, mid-range operations, PC support and helpdesk operations – rather than IT development and strategy.

However, whilst such statistics provide organizations with an indication of the areas in which the ITO market is likely to be more mature, each organization must make ITO decisions that best reflect its needs and particular circumstances rather than 'following the pack'. Imitative behaviour has long been noted to be a particular driver of ITO (Loh and Venkatraman, 1992) whereby organizations attempt to duplicate the imperfectly

Table 3.1 ITO decisions in Australia

	Not considered or N/A	Outsourcing rejected	Considering outsourcing	Partially outsourced	Fully outsourced
Mainframe and data centre operations					
Hardware support and maintenance	12%	4%	6%	34%	45%
Systems implementation	24%	3%	4%	60%	9%
Applications development	26%	10%	4%	42%	19%
Applications support and maintenance	27%	10%	5%	44%	14%
Systems integration	43%	9%	5%	32%	10%
Operations and facilities management	33%	18%	9%	21%	19%
Disaster recovery	40%	9%	12%	20%	18%
Client/server and desktop					
Hardware support and maintenance	11%	6%	7%	43%	34%
Systems implementation	20%	9%	6%	58%	8%
Applications development	27%	9%	5%	45%	13%
Applications support and maintenance	19%	11%	7%	50%	13%
Systems integration	39%	11%	7%	36%	7%
Operations and facilities management	38%	15%	11%	22%	14%
Disaster recovery	44%	11%	10%	24%	11%
IT management and support					
Education and training	15%	3%	5%	58%	19%
Helpdesk	36%	22%	13%	9%	19%
Asset management	63%	11%	7%	13%	6%
IT strategic planning	65%	21%	1%	13%	0%
Communications					
WAN services	9%	3%	7%	37%	44%
Operations and facilities management	31%	14%	10%	20%	24%
LAN services	36%	16%	10%	18%	20%

Source: Cullen *et al.* (2001), 233 respondents

observed success of others and the acclaimed gains, rather than strategically target the use of outsourcing in a manner focused on the unique needs and characteristics of the organization.

This building block is focused on helping organizations to target appropriate areas of IT activity from which the potential benefits of ITO can be gained, then to build a pragmatic base from which to approach ITO.

3.1 Select the suitable services

The objective of this activity is to identify the suitable tasks and services for outsourcing in a holistic manner across the entire IT portfolio of assets and activities, and package them appropriately. Any combination of IT services and technology platforms can be bundled for market testing. The organization's goal is to find the right combination to achieve the greatest benefits.

When determining whether or not an outsourcing arrangement is a workable option, also consider the following process. This process breaks out the services being considered into a techno-logical and service process format in which outsourcing criteria are applied in a systematic manner. From this, appropriate service packaging can occur.

Our recommended approach has five key steps:

Step	Description
1 Map the services	Break out the services into what is performed, where.
2 Establish the criteria	Identify short-term and long-term rationale for outsourcing, and the barriers against outsourcing.
3 Apply each criterion	Take each criterion independently and plot into the service map it applies to.
4 Aggregate the results	Aggregate each criterion into a total picture.
5 Determine priorities and service bundles	Organize the findings as to priority for outsourcing. From the map, determine which services it makes sense to bundle.

3.1.1 Map the services

To determine what service(s) have benefits that outweigh the barriers regarding ITO, the first step is to map out the services. This can take many forms. However, the critical objective is to break out what takes place (service process) from where it takes place (function).

- Service processes (or what takes place) are best described as the high level workflows under consideration.
- Functions (or where it takes place) can be quite broad (for example, divisions, geographical locations, user groups) or quite specific (technology, products, work units).

An IT function may be split as shown in Figure 3.1. The example is only meant to be suggestive, showing a range of services variously applied to the technical areas.

3.1.2 Determine the criteria for an outsourcing solution

Organizations often combine and convolute the reasons for and against outsourcing, never looking at the whole in a structured manner. Thus, we recommend that before determining which services to consider for outsourcing, determine the strategic goals for which outsourcing may be an optional solution, and also the barriers that will prevent successful outsourcing. In other words, develop a sourcing strategy as part of a business strategy, rather than think of IT outsourcing strategy in isolation.

The rationales worth looking at are of three types:

1 Short-term – benefits from outsourcing desired to occur almost immediately.
2 Long-term – benefits for outsourcing expected to occur over time and may need management to ensure that they do materialize.
3 Barriers – the risks that make outsourcing an inappropriate solution at this time.

The reasons why the organization is examining outsourcing now will be unique to the situation, and every examination performed within the organization will have different criteria that are applicable. However, Table 3.2 provides a 'shopping list' of generic criteria that has been used regularly in practice, from which an organization can determine its own specific criteria.

IT Technical Area						
	Infrastructure Platforms				Applications	
IT Service Area	Hardware Platform 1	Hardware Platform 2	Hardware Platform 3	Communications	Application 1	Application 2	Application 3
Appl'n development							
Appl'n support & maintenance							
Asset management							
Data centre facility & operations							
Disaster recovery							
Education							
Hardware support & maintenance							
Helpdesk							
IT strategy							
Systems implementation							
Systems integration							

Figure 3.1 Example IT service/technical matrix template

Table 3.2 General sourcing criteria list

Short-term objective criteria	Long-term objective criteria	Barrier criteria
Cost		
• **Cost savings** through introduction of competitive processes • **Cash flow** relief by selling assets and/or transferring staff • **Predictable costs** – through fixed or usage-based price models • **Transparency** – invoice is for all costs, avoiding trap of non-existent or inappropriate internal allocations • **Financial consequences** for inadequate performance	• **Efficiency motivation** by converting internal cost centre to a supplier profit centre • More **frugal use** of resources – when paying 'real' money, users change their behaviour	• **Process cost** of conducting the outsourcing project, transition and/or managing the supplier eliminates any savings and any strategic benefits • **Market price is higher** than internal cost • **Market is not competitive** – too few suppliers to create competitive tension, may have monopolist characteristics
Service		
• Access to leading edge, specialized **skills and/or technology** • **Guaranteed service levels** – expectations are contracted for • **Centralized support** – one point of call at the supplier • Match the level of asset/staff **supply to demand** to eliminate chronic over- or under-capacity • **Access to global** practices/technology/resources	• **Economies of scope** (variety of services able to be produced) • With pay for performance, suppliers are more **responsive to performance complaints** if it will affect profitability • **Gain innovative** ideas and techniques	• **Predictability** – requirements cannot be anticipated in any way • **Confidentiality** – data is so confidential no external party can have any dealings with it • **Failure** – risk of failure so high and mitigation strategies so poor, that the organization must perform the services itself • **Service knowledge is so specific** to that transferring that knowledge will create a monopoly • **The suppliers are immature** – inexperienced in the requirements

Investment

- **Access to technology** without capital investment
- **Shifting of expenditure** from the capital to the operating budget
- Eliminate **staff** shortages, skill gaps and continuous investment in recruiting and training

Organizational

- **Catalyst for organizational change** – behaviour, restructuring, rationalization, etc
- Remove **inflexible work practices**

- **Shorter lead times** to take advantage of new technology and ideas
- Enable **technology catching up** or leap-frogging – if converted to supplier's state-of-the-art infrastructure

- **Core focus** – concentrate resources on core/strategic initiatives
- **Customer focus** – concentrate on customers not operations

- **Assets are so specific** to the organization, transferring the knowledge to operate the assets will create a monopoly
- **Core competency or sustainable competitive advantage** is created by performing the services which must not be released into the market

- **Organization knowledge required** is so intricate that transferring such knowledge will create a monopoly
- **Organization is not ready** to outsource – skills, processes, knowledge

3.1.3 Applying the criteria and aggregating the results

When the map and the criteria have been developed, apply each criterion to each cell and determine if it is applicable to the area. Map each criterion separately – that is, use a blank matrix for each criterion. For example, if one of the criteria is to gain a core focus, then mark the cells where the organization most wants to gain this focus. This way each criterion is identified against the service and function where it is relevant.

Once aggregated, the results can resemble the bar graphs shown in Figures 3.2 and 3.3, as well as the matrix in Figure 3.4. Both of these techniques have been used successfully in practice over many years to determine and prioritize target activities for outsourcing.

In the above example, based on a real, if simplified case, if we look across the figures, the management-related and strategic planning processes are clearly not good candidates for outsourcing in their entirety as the barriers outweigh the desired

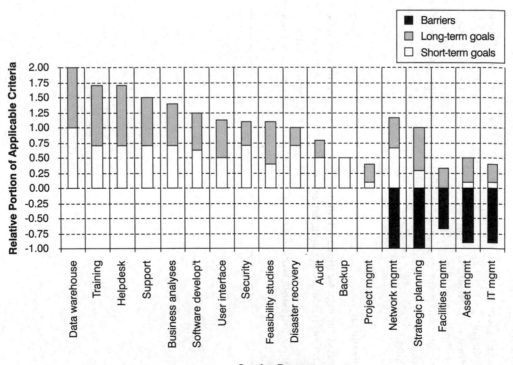

Figure 3.2 Example target services bar graph – service processes

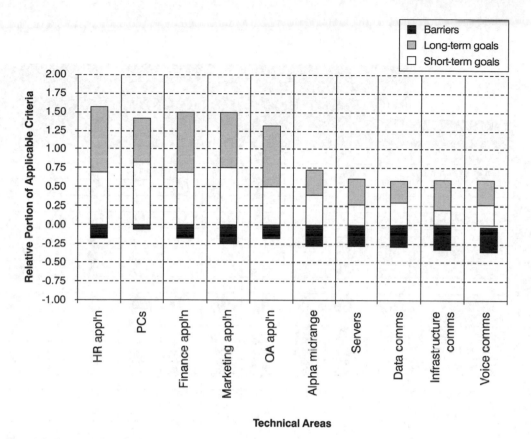

Figure 3.3 Example target services bar graph – technical areas

benefits. However, the rest of the processes are good candidates in varying degrees. From a technical or 'stovepipe' perspective, all the applications are good targets as well as the PCs. The benefits, while outnumbering the barriers, wane in comparison once communications and the midrange/server environments are considered.

In the event, the client chose a best-of-breed approach with a supplier providing desktop fleet management and the first level help desk (a study indicated the majority of calls were desktop-related), specialist providers to deliver the training, and an application specialist to develop, maintain and support the applications, data warehouse and user interfaces.

In Figure 3.5 we provide an outline of a target services report that documents the process and results of the assessment, and is designed to make the 'go forward' outsourcing decision transparent.

SERVICES	TECHNICAL AREAS									
	Hardware			Communications			Applications			
	PCs	Alpha	Servers	Infra-structure	Voice	Data	Marketing	Financial	HR	OA
Strategic Planning										
Feasibility Studies										
Business Analyses										
Software Development				n/a	n/a					
Data Warehouse				n/a	n/a	n/a				
User Interface				n/a	n/a					
Support										
IT Management										
Project Management										
Network Management							n/a	n/a	n/a	n/a
Facilities Management	n/a									
Asset Management										
Backup							n/a	n/a	n/a	n/a
Disaster Recovery										
Security										
Audit										
Training										
Help Desk										

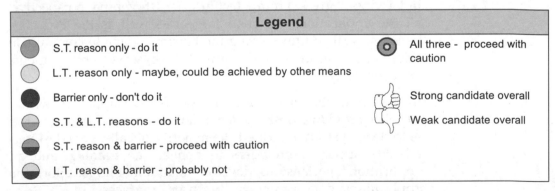

Legend

- S.T. reason only - do it
- L.T. reason only - maybe, could be achieved by other means
- Barrier only - don't do it
- S.T. & L.T. reasons - do it
- S.T. reason & barrier - proceed with caution
- L.T. reason & barrier - probably not
- All three - proceed with caution
- Strong candidate overall
- Weak candidate overall

Figure 3.4 Example target services matrix

1   Executive Summary

2   Introduction
    2.1   Background and Objectives
    2.2   Processes Undertaken
    2.3   Participants

3   Service Technical Areas & Processes Assessed
    3.1   Technical Categories
    3.2   Process Categories
    3.3   Matrix Shell

4   Criteria Used for the Evaluation
    4.1   Short-term Rationale/Objectives
    4.2   Long-term Rationale/Objectives
    4.3   Barriers to Outsourcing at this Time

5   Application of Criteria
    5.1   Short-term Criteria Applied
    5.2   Long-term Criteria Applied
    5.3   Barriers Criteria Applied

6   Aggregated Results
    6.1   Summary Matrix and Graphs
    6.2   Strong Targets for Outsourcing
    6.3   Weak Targets for Outsourcing
    6.4   Grey Areas - Inconclusive

7   Conclusions
    7.1   Findings
    7.2   Next Steps

Figure 3.5
Target services report
outline

3.2 Profile the target services

Once the target services have been identified, a detailed understanding of their current state is essential. The objective is to fully understand the nature and extent of each service that is being considered for outsourcing. Information such as baseline costs, and staff and customer profiles are collected at a high level for each service. Time and again we have found organizations skimping on this essential, foundational step, with deleterious consequences once outsourcing has occurred.

Some organizations make the mistake of assuming a service is standard or is well known, and therefore easy to put to the market without performing the necessary investigations to verify the current state. This fatal flaw has resulted in significant

1　Introduction
   1.1　Organizational Structure & Overview
   1.2　Strategic Plans
   1.3　Vision, Mission, Key Result Areas
   1.4　Service Environment

2　Services Profile
   2.1　Current service requirements
   2.2　Future service requirements
   2.3　Volume, trend and load data (number of users, transactions, desktops, helpdesk calls, etc)
   2.4　Performance criteria, service levels, measurement methods
   2.5　Customer satisfaction indices

3　Cost Profile
   3.1　Costs at current service levels
   3.2　Estimated costs at required or future service levels
   3.3　Future capital expenditure programme

4　Balance Sheet
   4.1　Assets (including intellectual property) – type, age, quantity, location
   4.2　Liabilities

5　Staff Profile
   5.1　Organization chart(s)
   5.2　Job descriptions
   5.3　Staff numbers and full time equivalents
   5.4　Remuneration
   5.5　Accrued and contingent liabilities

6　Commercial Relationships (contracts, licences, leases, etc)
   6.1　Scope
   6.2　Value
   6.3　End date
   6.4　Assignment and termination options

7　Stakeholder Profile
   7.1　Internal (users, departments)
   7.2　External (customers, suppliers, media)

8　Governance Profile
   8.1　Management
   8.2　Administration
   8.3　Control
   8.4　Reporting
   8.5　Systems

Figure 3.6 Services profile outline

cost increases when the actual scope of work is discovered, then redefined, by the successful supplier when there is no pressure to have competitive pricing. If an organization is currently performing a service, the time to find out what it is actually doing, what it owns, its obligations and so on are not after a supplier takes it over. Therefore undertake a close analysis, in a baseline period, of all present services and how they are delivered, and costs and standards of delivery, together with what benchmarks are being used. This is invaluable information for one's own piece of mind, but also for when dealing with the supplier's pitch on service delivery. Being fact-based is vital; this enables you to sit down and calculate, rather than have to negotiate in an ill-informed way, with the supplier.

We recommend that a services profile be developed after the identification of the target services, such that all future discussions, debates and strategies have a solid understanding of the key aspects of the service. This profile is necessary to provide an understanding of the services so that the organization can approach the market knowledgeably and minimize surprises later (which often increase costs). Aspects of this understanding will continue to develop over time.

The recommended services profile is made up of the components detailed in Figure 3.6. You will find such a document, properly researched, a hugely useful information source for subsequent dealings with the supplier.

3.3 Prepare the base case

The base case reflects the status quo case to which suppliers' bids will be compared against – typically the in-house cost adjusted for the cost and results of future strategies over the NPV (net present value) period. This is particularly useful if outsourcing is being tested for potential value for money ('market tested') rather than being executed as a strategy (in-house options will not be considered). It is also useful as the ongoing comparative if savings or other benefits are to be demonstrated over the life of the contract(s).

The base case takes the service profiles a step further. A comprehensive base case includes a rigorous examination of the current cost of the IT services along with the future projections, with particular emphasis on obtaining the often hidden and dispersed costs. Because of 'creative' internal accounting and budgeting mechanisms, organizations are not often in a position to know that the real costs are without highly detailed scrutiny. This is not easy, but well worth doing. For example, we have found as much as 40% of some organizations' IT expenditure to be in non-IT budgets. Tracing your real IT costs can be a real detective story! A true cost analysis includes a rigorous examination of your assumptions regarding the current cost of the IT services, with particular emphasis on obtaining hidden and dispersed costs.

For example, the following costs have often been found initially hidden in various places (note that this is merely a suggestive, not an exhaustive list):

- Data-centre costs hidden in facilities management
- Desktops and peripherals hidden in business unit budgets
- IT training buried in HR costs
- Consumable supplies (toner, diskettes, paper) in corporate purchasing
- On-site support (local 'experts') in the cost centres they report to.

Table 3.3 Base cost examples

	Examples:	
	Direct costs	**Indirect or overhead costs**
Labour	• Basic pay • Overtime • Bonuses • Training • Allowances • Superannuation	• Redundancy • Other compensation liabilities
IT Assets (equipment and software)	• Leases • Licences • Maintenance	
Accommodation	• Rent • Office machinery (faxes, copiers, telephones, etc) • Office furniture	• Utilities • Security • Cleaning
Operations	• Consumable supplies • Administration support	• Corporate department allocations (HR, accounting, legal, mail room, etc) • Insurances

Furthermore, if the IT organization is a centralized one it may be hit with allocated corporate overheads that are not reasonable allocations. For example, being allocated a portion of corporate marketing when it is not a revenue-generating business unit. These types of accounting arrangements need to be looked at very carefully and straightened out, if there is to be any chance of getting a true picture of in-house cost and service that can then be compared to a supplier bid on a like-for-like basis.

The organization's goal in developing the base case is to quantify the cost and outputs of the in-scope IT organization in a manner meaningful enough to make a comparison with the market price of obtaining the services over the foreseen term of the contract. Table 3.3 provides a suggested list for the major base costs you need to be looking for. The case study below details a not untypical event when one starts to look at IT costs more carefully – as you really have to do before outsourcing.

Case Study: a government agency

A national agency had scoped a very large potential ITO initiative. As part of its due diligence over the base case, it had conducted an inventory of IT service related activities and the staffing (FTEs – full-time equivalents) necessary to perform the services. In its originally scoped IT organization, it had documented one centralized IT helpdesk. During the base case development, it discovered that many of the business units had created their own helpdesks due to the poor customer service of the centralized function. The original FTE estimate of helpdesk-related staff tripled as a result.

3.4 Conduct the feasibility and impact study

The feasibility and impact study is one that some organizations choose to perform where the outsourcing being considered is high impact and high potential risk. Characteristics warranting such a study include if:

- it is one of the largest outsourcing initiatives undertaken by the organization;

- the market is inexperienced with an initiative of comparable size and/or scope, unfamiliar with the industry, and/or unproven with the nature of the desired relationship;
- the requirements, outputs and expectations are difficult to commercially articulate;
- the services are highly integrated within the organization and its value chain;
- leading edge technology is to be employed which has yet to prove itself in the industry, or significant modifications will be necessary to meet the organization's requirements; and/or
- a significant number of staff are likely to be transferred, or will no longer be required in the organization.

The types of issues to take into consideration, and to identify the potential impact and solutions for, include:

- Market capability to cover full scope – geographic, technological, service levels, etc.
- Future organizational direction and strategies – potential to favourably or adversely influence potential directions, including corporate structure changes (mergers, acquisitions, divestments), IT-enabled strategic initiatives (e-commerce, intranets, etc), customer care and so on.
- Human resources and employee relations – not just IT staff, but impact on the entire workforce.
- Integration with organizational business processes – in particular the inter-dependent 'handoff' points from a technological and workflow perspective.
- Corporate infrastructure (sites, facilities and assets) – identification of what will no longer be required and how the residual infrastructure can be affected.
- Corporate services – implications for resourcing and processes within corporate service departments (accounting, HR, property, etc).
- Corporate contracts – bulk purchase agreements, leases, insurances, etc.
- IT contracts – existing contracts which may require novation, assignment or termination.
- Conversion and transition requirements – technological (systems integration, firewalls, etc); HR (redundancies, transmission of business issues, etc); mobilization, knowledge and know-how transfer.

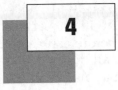
The fourth building block – ensure the results: design the future

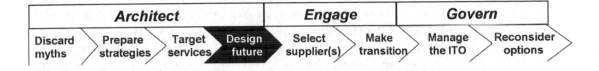

Architect				Engage		Govern	
Discard myths	Prepare strategies	Target services	Design future	Select supplier(s)	Make transition	Manage the ITO	Reconsider options

This building block, designing the future, builds on the previous blocks to convert the desired arrangement into a commercially sound framework. This block covers the detailed design of the arrangement, and precedes the selection process because, logically, accepting a bid for an ill-defined product is unsound practice. The contract and SLA, in particular, are the organization's formal 'product' specification documents. They must be detailed at some point. Leaving it until later means that the supplier has a greater opportunity to drive the process – which may not be in the organization's best interest.

This framework includes developing the:

- future arrangement vision;
- legal obligations, rights and recourse via the contract;
- service specifications, key performance indicators and result-ant remedy/reward scheme and reporting requirements via the service level agreement; and
- retained organization and contract management.

Too often, we have seen organizations disappointed that some of their expectations have not been met (for example, the introduction of innovations from other customers, exposure to global expertise, access to the latest research and development initiatives). However, these expectations were never articulated and agreed to, let alone a plan devised for meeting them. The benefits sought by outsourcing are not inherent in the act of outsourcing. They must be designed to occur.

Organizations must not allow ITO to be ideologically driven – assuming that acclaimed benefits are inherent in the act of outsourcing, and that what others have done before can easily be replicated. An organization will never know all the facts that made another organization's deal successful, may not be in the same position (for example, the other deal may have been a loss-leader for the supplier), may not be in the same market, may not have the same organizational and cost structure, and may not even be outsourcing the same mix of activities.

Nonetheless, outsourcing as an imitative behaviour rather than a well thought out strategy still occurs. Researchers at MIT (Massachusetts's Institute of Technology) studied 60 US contracts from 1985 to 1990, finding that Kodak's act of outsourcing started the prevailing push for outsourcing. In this case, the prominence of the organizations involved (Kodak, IBM, DEC, etc) and the size of the contract ($500 million) gave a higher level of visibility than existed before. Kodak, as an opinion leader, was a symbol of legitimacy to potential adopters and so the imitation process began. This finding led the researchers to name the outsourcing bandwagon that subsequently occurred as the 'Kodak Effect'. Envious organizations attempted to duplicate the imperfectly observed feat without achieving the expected results, because it was not the act of outsourcing in isolation that drove success. For example, Kodak's cost savings are still quoted; however what is not quoted are the five studies they performed, each six to nine months in duration, before the outsourcing decision was made and the years of organizational re-engineering that took place in preparation to make outsourcing work. Furthermore, the subsequent history of those historic deals is rarely discussed, even though in fact parts of the deal with three suppliers proved not that successful at all.

4.1 Vision the attributes of the future arrangement

Arrangement modelling comprises developing the future vision for how the relationship, governing documents and the entire outsourcing framework is to work. It is a cyclical process that is refined throughout the lifecycle and, in fact, never ceases as new information and requirements come to bear.

The types of design elements to start visioning at the onset are summarized in Figure 4.1, while Table 4.1 breaks down these elements into sample questions to answer and gives examples of desired outputs from the design process. In this section we felt

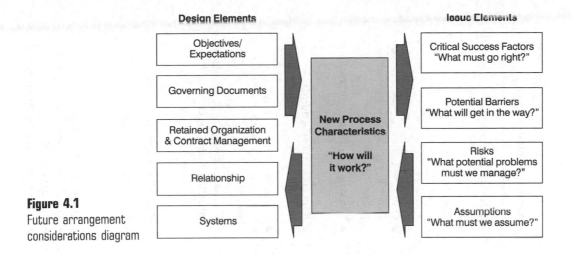

Figure 4.1
Future arrangement
considerations diagram

it most useful to provide much of the material in tabular and checklist form so that these can be used fairly directly by practitioners.

The checklist in Table 4.2 provides a snapshot of the key elements of a best practice outsourcing arrangement. Each organization will need to create its own checklist that represents the high level attributes it prefers to see in the outsourcing arrangement. For those thinking initially that these practices read a little idealistically, we can confirm that we have seen and participated in deals that exhibited many of these practices.

4.2 Develop the service level agreement and key performance indicators

The service level agreement (SLA) is the definition of what successful service will be. It defines the expectations, being prescriptive only when necessary, sets the key performance criteria and much more. An SLA imposes a service commitment on both sides – the supplier to provide defined services with defined performance, and the customer to use those services within defined parameters. This depersonalizes service review meetings and leads to an objective evaluation of performance by both parties.

SLAs force organizations to define service and develop appropriate performance measures, if only as a means to ensure contractual compliance. As such, it is not necessarily outsourcing that can produce a better service, but the definition

Table 4.1 Future arrangement example questions and outputs

Design elements	Example questions to answer	Example potential outputs
Objectives/ expectations	What is the organization seeking to accomplish by outsourcing (i.e. skills, technology, cost savings)?	• Outsourcing success measurements
	Can the organization identify a cost threshold that the market price must be less than (will prevent outsourcing)?	• Cost threshold
Governing documents	What will be the key documents employed to govern the commercial understanding? What is the best structure of the documents?	• Outlines: Contract, SLA, Price Model • Other key schedules – baselines, guarantees, etc
	Who should be involved in their development? Does the organization have all the skills required?	• Working group(s) identification
	How often might they be required to be refreshed?	• Renegotiation schedule
Retained organization and arrangement management	What is the rationale for retaining services vs. outsourcing? What is likely to be retained in the organization (services, skills, number of personnel)?	• Sourcing criteria • Retained organization structure and budget
	What sort of relationship/contract management (skills, number of personnel) does the organization expect? What are the key activities?	• Contract management organization structure and budget
Relationship	What is the vision for the ideal relationship?	• Shared relationship values
	How often and what type of interaction is envisioned? What management investment (type, budget) is the organization willing to put into the supplier(s)?	• Partnering program
	What sort of supplier behaviour does the organization expect? How can the organization ensure that the behaviour will occur? How does the organization expect the supplier to manage the customer account?	• Model of 'ideal' supplier • Initial list of potential suppliers • Evaluation criteria • Customer reference questions

Systems

What integration and security is likely to be required between the supplier(s) and the organization? What systems/subsystems does the organization wish the supplier to use vs. their own or preferred system(s)?

- Integration requirements
- Security requirements

Critical success factors
'What must go right?'

Are there stakeholders that must 'buy into' the project and/or outsourcing in general?

Are there deadlines that must be met?

What skills/services must the supplier(s) excel at? What are mandatory vs. 'nice to have' capabilities?

- Stakeholder management plan
- Milestones
- Mandatory requirements

Barriers
'What may get in the way?'

Are there any issues that may stop the outsourcing initiative? What are the 'no go' decision stoplights?

- 'Go/no go' criteria

Risks
'What risks must we manage?'

Are there lifecycle resource constraints (skills, availability, etc)?

What are the 'unknowns' about what the organization is seeking (best practice, price, technology, etc)?

- Project contingency planning
- Issue log

Assumptions
"What must we assume?'

What assumptions might the organization need to make regarding potential structural changes during the term of the contract (mergers, acquisitions, divestment, reorganization, etc)? What assumptions might the organization need to make regarding new/modified systems? What are the best/worst/most likely scenarios for demand (capacity, staff, etc)?

- Potential changes to the organization systems, etc during the term of the contract
- Scenario planning

Table 4.2 Attributes of a best practice outsourcing arrangement checklist

Relationship (both parties)
- Mutual respect and trust
- Willingness to work hard together
- Continuous improvement
- Proactive and reactive to other party's needs/concerns
- Regular and ongoing monitoring and evaluation
- Frequent and open communications
- Works seamlessly with all parties
- Clear protocols

Supplier
- Deliver 'promises' made during lifecycle, particularly during the selection process
- Client needs are sought and addressed
- Satisfaction is assessed and actioned
- Honest in reporting
- Seek opportunities to solve business issues

Client
- Recognizes supplier's right to make a profit
- Communication of business goals, issues, manner of operating
- Early warning of major issues impacting the services
- Prompt payment
- Smart and regular planning
- Involvement of supplier in planning process
- No abdication of responsibilities

Financial
- Demonstrates value for money and competitiveness at regular intervals
- Level of transparency enabling the organization to assess cost drivers and react accordingly
- Trends following general industry trends
- KPIs improving over time within same price or price reducing over time within same KPIs

Contractual/–service level agreement
- Air-tight contract (safety net), performance based SLA (definition of success), 'partnering' style relationship
- Flexibility to add and remove services ('chop and change')
- Not exclusive to one supplier but allows flexibility to have different suppliers for out of scope/additional services if deemed best of breed or better value
- Regular and meaningful reporting
- Balanced scorecard approach to performance – measuring the few truly critical KPIs that drive the perception of value, not everything that can be measured
- Incentives to exceed expectations in key areas, recourse if below expectations
- Outcome/output based expectations, prescriptive only when required
- Aim to be fair – have underlying tone of partnering, not overtly adversarial

Technical
- Flexibility on platforms, hardware, software
- Reliable and predictable services
- Hardware/software at industry standard (current release) or industry standard minus 1? (previous release)
- Matching of supply and demand (minimize mismatch between capacity and need)
- Appropriate skill sets
- Able to bring value-added services Has access to global knowledge and resources

and measurement processes that go with it. SLAs as a management tool are available to internal service providers. However, they are not as common, nor frequently are they as well enforced, thus giving an external provider a competitive advantage. As one IT director said of his internal SLA regime and cost/performance arrangements, 'in truth it felt a little like playing at shops'.

As our study in Australia noted (Figure 4.2), over 60% of organizations did not have any form of internal SLAs. However, only 11% did not have SLAs with their external providers. This may well reflect in-house reluctance to embark on a difficult set of tasks. In fact an effective SLA is one of the most difficult governance documents to produce for any IT arrangement (Cullen *et al.*, 2001), because in particular it involves determining the service levels and anticipating future needs and changes to the service requirements. Even under much greater pressure to get these right as a result of outsourcing, 29% of organizations still experienced serious/difficult problems getting service definitions and levels right, according to Lacity and Willcocks (2001). Only 14% of organizations found this area 'not a problem'.

An SLA is a schedule to the contract, and hence part of the legal framework. However, it is crucial for it to be written in the

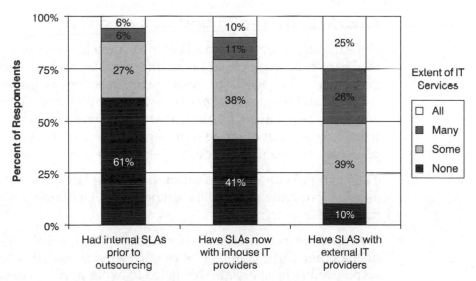

Source: Cullen et al (2001); 227, 188 and 199 respondents respectively

Figure 4.2 SLA use – internal vs external

language of the service rather than 'legalese'. How the contract and SLA fit together is shown below:

Contract:	SLA (schedule to the contract):

• Spells out legal:
  – Obligations, rights and responsibilities
  – Guarantees, liabilities, recourse.
  – Renewal and termination options.
	• Spells out service:
	  – Requirements and expectations.
	  – Definitions, KPIs and measures.
	  – Relationships.

• Should be air-tight and referred to in limited circumstances (dusty).	• Should be in use and under constant change (living).
• Written for problems.	• Written for success.

To help the learning practitioner, we also provide the outline of a typical SLA in Figure 4.3, including the main headings under which it can be drawn up.

The remainder of this SLA section discusses the key area of SLAs in further detail, including:

• defining the scope and services;
• performance measurement regimes;
• reporting and management.

4.2.1 Defining in and out of scope

Once the target services have been determined as recommended in Chapter 2, disaggregation of the services should occur to determine what work processes are 'in-scope' (will be out-sourced) and what work processes are 'out of scope' (performance will be retained by the client organization). The total of what is in and out of scope represents the totality of what work processes are involved in delivering the service.

The in and out of scope definition in its simplest form is merely a table identifying who will be doing what. An example is given in Table 4.3.

We recommend that organizations adopt the principle that one or the other party is in charge of each service, and that shared responsibility be avoided. This helps to avoid doubt as to whom is to do what. If both parties share accountability, the likelihood of blame displacement increases dramatically. Accordingly, one

1   Background and purpose of this SLA
    1.1   Background
    1.2   Objectives
    1.3   Customers and stakeholders
    1.4   Format of this SLA

2   Services in Scope and Out of Scope
    2.1   Scope/responsibility matrix
    2.2   Service interdependencies and related responsibilities
    2.3   Potential variations (optional)
    2.4   Value-added opportunities/services (optional)

3   In Scope Service Description (for each service)
    3.1   Overview/description/requirements
    3.2   Basic requirements
    3.3   Objectives/critical success factors

4   Performance Measurement Regime
    4.1   Key Performance Indicators (KPIs)
    4.2   Service fee adjustments (recourse, bonuses)
    4.3   Point at which performance invokes the right to terminate/extend (optional)

5   Reporting
    5.1   Performance (KPI) reports
    5.2   Operating reports (volumes, usage, capacity, etc)
    5.3   Progress/status reports (projects, changes, improvements, etc)
    5.4   Incident/exception reports

6   Governance
    6.1   Structure
    6.2   Roles and responsibilities
    6.3   Meetings and reviews
    6.4   Evaluations, reviews and audits
    6.5   Communications framework
    6.6   Management procedures (problem escalation, variations, etc)

7   Glossary

Appendices

Figure 4.3 Example SLA outline

party has the lead and the other has a contributory role in the event that both need to work together. This is not a small point. We have witnessed plenty of long drawn-out struggles over service performance where responsibilities were not clarified at an early stage.

Table 4.3 Example scope table (partial)

Services	SLA ref	Description	In-scope	Out-of-scope
1 Strategic Services		IT Business Unit Management		X
		IT Strategy		X
		IT Standards Development		X
2 Mainframe Service Group	#.#	Provision of, support for, and maintenance of specified Mainframe facilities	X	
3 Disaster Recovery Planning (DRP) Service Group	#.#	DRP for the Mainframe and specified Unix servers	X	
		DRP for NT Servers and Lotus Notes servers		X

4.2.2 In-scope service definitions

Once the in-scope services are known, the task of defining what the organization intends the supplier to provide can begin.

One of the contributing factors to dissatisfaction on the part of the customer occurs when the supplier misinterprets the service definitions provided by the customer. This is easily done. Most service specifications are typically written by in-house staff who assume far too much and do not articulate the services in a commercially sufficient manner. The supplier's misinterpretation is more often than not genuine, it is rarely an overt attempt to increase the price (albeit out-of-scope charges can be one result). For this reason, it is important for the client representatives to focus on getting clear words that are quite common to both parties, but that may have different meaning within each party. For example, something as simple as business hours has caused disputes, when not clearly specified, as the parties had different business hours. Anything not reasonably defined (i.e. an independent reasonable party would interpret the meaning the same regardless of either party's perspective) has the greatest likelihood to attract out-of-scope charges.

The service definitions do not function as an operational procedures manual, and therefore do not detail how tasks are to be performed. There may be instances where the organization must specify the exact process, but we recommend that caution be used whenever being didactic, as the prescription must be

The Contractor will provide a system to log Incidents. The Contractor shall receive and log all calls raised by the Customer's and the Contractor's staff. The general scope of the Call Logging Function shall include, but not be limited to, the following:

1 Log the Incident in a central database allocating a unique reference.

2 Record the following information:
 • Unique Incident Number
 • Name of User
 • User Category, Business Unit and Location
 • Incident Category
 • Description of the Incident
 • Area/Person currently assigned to resolve the Incident
 • Resolution actions performed to date
 • Status of the Incident (e.g. Open, Resolved, Closed)
 • Date/Time Incident: Reported, Resolved, Closed
 • Any other details as agreed by the Customer.

3 Assign an Incident Priority as per the table in HelpDesk Manual. The Incident Priority for any particular Incident will be agreed between the Customer and the Contractor at the time of problem logging.

4 Advise the caller of the following details:
 • Unique Incident Number
 • Incident Priority
 • Next steps in process
 • Approximate timings of response/resolution.

5 Notify other Users if the Incident may affect other users – communicating the issue, the likely cause and estimated resolution time to those affected Users.

6 Notify the Customer CIO of all Incidents not fixed in specified resolution time.

Figure 4.4 Example service description – call logging

complete and comprehensive or out-of-scope charges are probable. Being precise can be a strength if you are working from full information, but a weakness if you are not! Accordingly, when using lists ensure that they are explicitly 'including but not limited to' lists and meant to illustrate the type of tasks that comprise the service, but do not prescribe all the tasks. Figure 4.4 provides a sample service description for call logging.

4.2.3 Key performance indicators (KPIs)

KPIs are designed to drive the behaviour of the supplier as they represent the 'report card' metrics that the supplier will be held accountable to, reported on and compared to other organizations with. Accordingly, it is important to ensure the KPIs are truly key drivers of performance expectations, not just 'nice to know'.

Furthermore, they should reflect what good service is in the eyes of the stakeholders. Many organizations make the mistake of simply collecting measurements that are easy to capture. These do not always reflect what the stakeholders really care about, nor do they reflect how these stakeholders perceive good service.

Case Study: a telecommunications organization

A major telco was outsourcing for the first time and had little in the way of KPIs for the in-house service providers. A working group was formed of users and internal service providers to determine what KPIs should be in an externally provided SLA. After months of work, the final outcome was 70 KPIs, due to the discomfort the team felt regarding outsourcing and the potential lack of control. While these were somewhat prioritized by the number of 'penalty points' that were attracted for each percentage drop from the KPI minimum standard, both organizations spent enormous effort in putting in place the measurement and reporting systems. Even so, neither party could quickly determine whether the 'contract was successful' at any given point without extensive analysis of the 70 KPIs.

It is because of inappropriate measures (not measuring the right things) that we have observed suppliers believing they are doing a great job, which is demonstrable according to their achievement of the specified KPIs, while at the same time the customer stakeholders are dissatisfied, and may even come to hold the supplier in contempt.

A customer or user satisfaction survey, while often incorporated into the KPI framework, can also be a useful, separate indicator as to whether the organization is measuring the customer's perception of good service. If the reported KPIs are showing high achievement, but the satisfaction survey is highlighting dissatisfied customers, one cause could be that wrong measurements are in place. The other cause is often that the customers have not been educated as to what they should expect pertinent to what has been agreed and paid for, thus they may have higher expectations than the agreement warrants.

The onus is, firstly, on the customer to articulate what will satisfy their requirements. The process of determining KPIs should begin with the stakeholders to determine foremost what is most important for them in terms of successful service delivery. Figure 4.5 outlines the core process of arriving at this understanding.

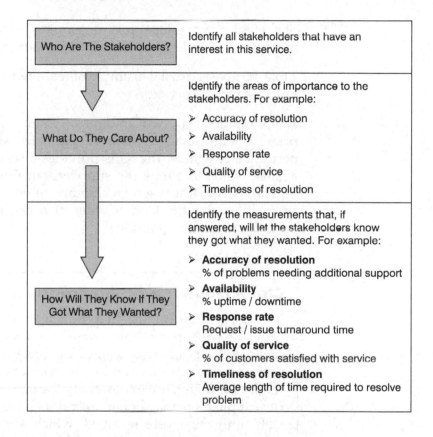

Figure 4.5
Determining what is important to stakeholders

Once the organization has defined how the stakeholders will perceive good service, then it can set about ensuring that their expectations will be delivered by:

1 Articulating KPI measures that are:
  • relevant – to the scope of the supplier's control;
  • readily available – from systematically collected data;
  • reliable – replicable measurement systems; and
  • simple and understandable – to the stakeholders.
2 Designing the measurement system including the:
  • source data – objective and auditable source of the KPI information; and
  • reports – how the information should be presented and aggregated.

3 Designing the financial incentive programme:
- rebates – for substandard performance whereby the KPIs have not been achieved, including financial and option to terminate; and
- bonuses – for performance above specifically identified KPIs or achievement of KPIs set up as targets.

The eight major steps for developing such a performance measurement system are described in Table 4.4.

Table 4.5 gives a partial example of real-life KPIs, in this case for on-site support services.

We recommend a good amount of testing of the KPI system prior to outsourcing wherever possible. Measuring current performance against the KPIs provides a service level baseline against which to gauge the supplier, but this also enables the organization to test potential circumvention. The following case study illustrates the kind of thing that can happen, and why proper testing is a good idea.

Case Study: a government agency

The outsourcing of the helpdesk had led to remarkable improvements in resolution times. As a result, outsourcing of other IT services was deemed the preferred option where service was inadequate and many services were put out to tender. However, unbeknownst to the customer agency and the supplier's management, operators were not logging the calls until they were resolved, which directly resulted in extraordinary resolution times. This came about due to two factors: (1) to save money, an automated system had not been installed, thus proper recording was the responsibility of the operator, and (2) the supplier gave operators bonuses if they exceeded KPIs, primarily that of call resolution times. The operators quickly determined that these call resolution KPIs could easily be exceed by waiting to log the call, solving the problem, then recording the log date and resolution date. This was discovered a year after the contract was awarded when an astute auditor queried why the operators were so busy manually writing things down rather than keying data into a system, an occurrence which is unusual in 'best practice' helpdesks.

Table 4.4 Eight steps for developing KPIs

Step	Actions
1 *Set scope parameters*	a) Confirm in-scope services b) Define span of supplier's control c) Define business process 'breaks' where supplier's span of control does not represent an end-to-end process
2 *Define stakeholders for each service*	a) Identify who cares about each service b) Identify what each stakeholder cares about, what they are depending upon the supplier to deliver
3 *Identify critical success factors*	a) Determine the minimum crucial determinants that each SLA stakeholder group will use to determine whether 'good service' has been received b) Determine what would be the minimum expectation and also complete service failure for each SLA stakeholder group c) Determine what would delight for each SLA stakeholder group if the minimum expectation was exceeded
4 *Generate performance measures appropriate to each stakeholder group that are …*	a) readily available (the source data is obtainable in a cost effective manner), b) simple and understandable (minimize convolution), c) relevant (tied to critical success factors), d) reliable (minimal 'noise' or supplier uncontrollable variables that can interfere with the measure), e) complete (add to 100%), and f) actionable (response required to improve performance are identifiable)
5 *Set thresholds*	a) Set minimum performance required (bottom line) b) Set performance goals to be strived for (top line) c) Determine impact and actions/desired rights regarding non-achievement
6 *Design measurement and reporting system*	a) Prototype performance reports including trends and segmentation b) Identify how and from where performance data will be sourced
7 *Walkthrough the system*	a) Obtain current measurements (baselines) b) Predict desired (expected) behaviours c) Predict potentially undesired behaviours that may result
8 *Build commitment*	a) Assign accountabilities b) Design performance review program c) Develop results communication plan d) Design feedback/continuous improvement procedures

Table 4.5 Example KPIs (partial)

Service Area	KPI	Service level
Specified On-Site Support Services	Availability of On-site Support Contact – Critical	Available to provide support <30 mins for 100% of Critical Requests
	Availability of On-site Support Contact – All Other Requests	• Available to provide support <1 hour for 80% of All Other Requests • Available <4 hours for remaining 20% of All Other Requests
	Device Relocation	• >95% within 48 hours • 100% within 72 hours
	Installation of SOE Device	• >95% within 48 hours • 100% within 72 hours

To help guide the stakeholders in articulating their perceptions of value, consider a balanced scorecard approach. This attempts to reflect more comprehensive success criteria of an ITO arrangement via a portfolio of KPIs (see Figure 4.6). Service quality (the most common type of measurement in most SLAs) is a key component, but not the only one. In Table 4.6 we give a detailed example of the balanced scorecard concept as applied to an IT outsourcing arrangement. (A more full treatment of balanced scorecards can be found in a companion volume in this series – Willcocks and Greaser (2001), *Delivering IT and E-Business Value*.)

Service	Relationship
• Quality • Consistency (across geographies, customer bases)	• Values • Responsiveness • Proactivity
Price	**Strategic**
• History against baseline • Competitiveness • Transparency • TCO (total cost of ownership)	• Objectives achievement • Innovation • Business contribution • Society contribution

Figure 4.6
Balanced scorecard

Design the future

Table 4.6 Example balance scorecard measures

Category	Description	Example measures
Service	Service quality KPIs are the minimum to include as they represent the fundamental success of service delivery	• Accuracy – data entry, reports • Availability – uptime/downtime, abandon rates • Completeness – data, tasks, reports • Efficiency – processing rate, volumes • Response rates – service initiation, turnaround time, resolution rate • Timeliness – deadlines
Price	Price/cost KPIs are next in consideration as they complete the value for money equation	• History compared to baseline – ongoing reduction in costs or steady costs but improving services • Competitiveness – compared to current market rates • Transparency (cost per unit of demand or input) – detailed and matched to cost drivers • TCO (total cost of ownership) – contribution towards reducing entire IT costs
Relationship	Relationship KPIs measure the health of the relationship, which is often a leading indicator of the potential for service or price issues	• Service – recourse unnecessary, bonuses achieved. Services of consistent high standard, comparable to market standards, and customers delighted • Financial – parties achieve financial goals • Communication – communicate frequently, openly and honestly • Meet needs – proactive and reactive to other party's needs • Creative solutions – continuously search for better ways of doing things • Conflict – parties focus on solving the problem, not apportioning blame. Resolve conflict at the lowest level • Fairness – parties fair to each other • Time – provide each other time and management focus • External relations – parties project a united front and do not discuss sensitive issues outside the relationship • Industry model – relationship seen as an industry model • Enjoyment – enjoy working together and respect one another • Technology leadership – recognized technology leadership
Strategic	Strategic KPIs are those high-level metrics that go beyond the letter of the agreement	• Degree ITO objectives achieved – statistical, perception • Business contribution – organization achieved more out of the relationship than just an exchange of cash for services. Can be joint offerings to the market, sharing of R&D initiatives, knowledge transfer, etc • Society contribution – industry development, research, greening

83

4.2.4 Rebate/bonus schemes

Penalties[1] and rewards encourage suppliers to deliver to expectations and, where desired, to deliver outstanding service. The general premise is that the price of the services will require adjustments based on the quality received. Penalties are an accepted practice now and are more common than rewards. However, there is an increasing use of rewards (Cullen *et al.*, 2001) and suppliers are increasingly very active regarding the inclusion of incentives in service contracts.

At a minimum, KPIs set the base-level standard of service level to be achieved, which may have recourse for failure. Not all KPIs will necessary attract a 'penalty'. However, if one does not, the importance of that KPI should be queried. Many organizations separate KPIs from PIs (performance indicators as opposed to key performance indicators) and only have a financial scheme over the KPIs. In this manner, measurements of interest to certain stakeholders or 'second tier' measurements can be obtained systematically. More complex KPI schemes have performance targets as well, which may be rewarded (via financial or contract extension incentives) if achieved.

With rewards, the increased levels of service delivered should bring about a business benefit, but it is often difficult to measure the business benefit gained without a direct link to the actions of the supplier. In practice, rewards have worked best when target KPIs have been set for the few services that have value to the organization if the supplier exceeds minimum KPIs. Examples include the reduction of helpdesk calls, clearance of backlog application change requests, improved desktop installation times, and higher customer satisfaction ratings.

With regard to the use of penalties, organizations can lose sight of the central purpose, namely to direct the behaviour of the supplier. The goal of a penalty scheme should never be to actually obtain the penalties, but rather to ensure that minimum expectations are met. In this spirit, some organizations elect to allow the supplier to 'clawback' penalties if subsequent performance is good. The reverse is true of rewards, the purpose of

---

[1] While we use the word penalties to refer to financial compensation for poor service, we recommend each organization apply a different term as it has a special meaning in the courts (genuine pre-estimate of loss) that is not applicable here. Replacement terms include: liquidated damages, fee adjustments, incentives, rebates, credits, etc.

which is to have the supplier achieve and sustain them. The sometimes strange relationship between reward/penalty systems and behaviour is illustrated by the following case study.

Case Study: a regional bank

The management over the outsourcing of IT services had been delegated to the finance department of a small regional bank. As IT was outsourced, it was considered now to be primarily a procurement issue rather than a service issue. The finance depart had little IT experience, but knew how to 'extract value' from procurement contracts. Accordingly, it set a budget for the achievement of penalties and in this manner it believed it would demonstrate prudent financial management by continuously reducing IT costs. The development of processes and resolution of service issues giving rise to such penalties were never considered. In fact, the contract manager had a personal goal to achieve penalties at least equal to his salary. Over time, the bank eventually brought all the services back in-house as outsourcing was deemed to result in inadequate control over service quality.

Egalitarian customer organizations have set up penalty schemes over their own responsibilities as well (for example, for late approvals). While we have not observed this as a frequent occurrence, it is one worth considering where the success of an IT service depends as much on the organization doing its part as it does on the suppliers doing theirs.

The application of incentives and penalties can occur via several means. In each case, the amount of penalties and/or rewards is typically, but not always, limited to the 'at-risk' amount. Table 4.7 describes three bonus/rebate approaches – fixed amount, percent and points, while Table 4.8 provides an example of a percent based rebate approach. Here, failure to achieve the monthly KPIs results in a rebate commensurate with the percentages listed against the fixed 'at-risk' amount.

Some organizations choose to escalate the 'penalty' scheme if substandard performance continuously re-occurs either in consecutive periods or, for example, three months out of six. An example of this is provided in Table 4.9.

4.2.5 Termination for poor SLA performance

At some stage, as a last resort, the organization may want the right to terminate a service for poor performance by the supplier. This may be because either of the following occurred:

- a failure so significant and probability of re-occurrence so high; or
- prolonged under performance of one or more KPIs (say three consecutive months, or six months out of twelve).

To deal with the organization's rights for such redress, the SLA should specify at what point continuation of the services is no longer desirable from the organization's standpoint. The organization may want the right to terminate only that service which is under performing, known as partial termination, if separation of the related services is viable. Termination of the entire contract may be a desirable right for key services that cannot be separated off individually.

This right can be powerful without having to be executed. A loaded gun does not have to be fired to be a convincing persuader! It provides the organization with strong negotiation power over the supplier, to put in other resolutions, or improve the arrangement to keep the service portfolio intact. An example of such a termination provision is shown in Figure 4.7.

In addition to any other rights it has to terminate this Agreement, the Client may, in its absolute discretion, terminate this Agreement in whole or in part with respect to any one or more Services if the supplier:

(a) incurs 100% of the Service Fee Adjustment in each month over a continuous period of at least 3 months; or

(b) incurs 100% of the Service Fee Adjustment in each month for 5 months out of a rolling twelve month period; or

(c) fails to deliver a Service in accordance with the Service Levels set out for that Service in the SLA for 3 consecutive months.

Figure 4.7 Example termination provision for KPI failure

4.2.6 Reporting

There will be a number of reports any organization that has outsourced will require, and a number of stakeholders will want certain information. The main categories of reports are:

1 Performance reports – each KPI minimum standard agreed, the actual level achieved, the variance between them and any resultant rewards/penalties.
2 Operating reports – the statistics necessary to keep abreast of what is happening operationally, for example in workload, volumes of transactions, number of hours worked, etc.
3 Progress reports – updating the organization on the status of work in progress, projects, the continuous improvement agenda, etc.

Table 4.10 provides a partial example of reporting requirements within an SLA.

Table 4.10 Example reporting requirements (partial)

Reports		Frequency	Format and contents
Performance	1 KPIs	Monthly	Report on all KPIs, actual to minimum and the variance for current period and 6 month rolling period
Operating	2 Access Management a) Number of access requests and resets	Monthly	Current period and 6 month trend
	b) Security violations	Monthly	Current period and 6 month trend
	3 Capacity	Quarterly	Capacity trends, growth projections and recommendations
	4 Problems	Monthly	For each problem severity, number of problems reported and number corrected and 6 month trend
Progress	5 Projects	Monthly	• Project name • Date project approved, project start and end times • % completed, work (hours) to complete • Budgeted cost, actual cost to date, estimated cost to complete • Items exposing project • Items awaiting action

4.2.7 Relationship management

The purpose of this section within an SLA is to outline how the relationship between the supplier and the organization is to be managed. It is comprised of laying out the:

● Relationship structure.
● Roles and accountabilities.
● Meetings.

The relationship structure can be as simple as an organization chart for managing the SLA (see Figure 4.8).

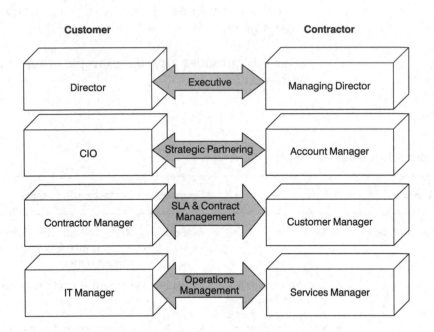

Figure 4.8
Example relationship structure

Typically the roles and accountabilities follow, articulating the responsibilities that each member of each party's SLA management team have. Table 4.11 provides an example. These structures provide much needed clarity in, and control over, relationships, without which events like the one detailed in the insurance company case study below become more likely.

Table 4.11 Example relationship roles/responsibilities

Customer role	Responsibility
Director	Responsible for overall strategic partnership between the Customer and the Contractor
CIO	Responsible for the overall commercial relationship between the Customer and the Contractor
Contractor Manager	Responsible for ensuring performance of the Agreement between the Customer and the Contractor
IT Manager	Responsible for assisting the Contractor Manager and managing day-to-day operational and technical issues

Contractor role	Responsibility
Managing Director	Responsible for the executive and commercial relationship between the Contractor and the Customer
Account Manager	Responsible for overall strategic partnering relationship between the Contractor and the Customer
Customer Manager	Responsible for providing the resources and skills to deliver the requirements of the contract and SLA
Services Manager	Acts as a single point of contact for the Contractor and is a direct interface to the Customer at an operational level for all technical, logistic and support issues. Responsible for: 1 Tracking service delivery against the SLA 2 Facilitating regular communication and reporting, including regular review meetings 3 The overall scope of work on behalf of all of the Contractor's parties involved in service delivery 4 Maintaining an 'Information Repository' of communications and documentation relating to the Services, which is available to all nominated Customer personnel

---

Case Study: an insurance company

An organization that outsourced had its costs blow out 500% from the previous year. After a brief analysis, the root cause was determined to be due to the lack of control over the relationship. Anyone in either organization could contact anyone in the other party. Thus, staff were requesting and getting many more services than were provided for in the contract and the supplier never said no. In fact, the supplier quickly realized it could offer many services and the organization's staff would never say no.

It was precisely to stop such events from occurring that the contract facilitator role, described in Chapter 1, developed over time in many deals. A number of meetings will be required to successfully manage the client–supplier arrangements. The frequency of meetings and seniority of attendees can depend on:

- the maturity of the arrangement;
- whether KPIs are being met;
- commercial value of the arrangement;
- how close the contract is up for renewal;
- degree of potential changes to either party's business;
- degree of proposed changes to the services; and
- nature, number and importance of projects in process.

An example of a SLA meetings schedule is provided in Table 4.12.

At a minimum, consider:

- strategic planning meetings in line with the business planning cycle;
- performance meetings in line with the timing of the performance reporting;
- pre-invoice meetings if invoices will vary from period to period and the amounts could be subject to debate; and
- more frequent operational meetings.

Also consider regular 'partnering' workshops and continuous improvement meetings. Some meetings are not just to solve issues, but forge a 'partnering' style relationship regardless of the nature of the contract. If the parties aren't meeting regularly, they may not be talking enough.

Table 4.12 Example meetings schedule

continued

Frequency	Meeting	Attendees	Topics
Annual	1 Balanced Scorecard Review	*Customer Representatives:* • CIO • Contractor Manager *Contractor Representatives:* • Account Manager • Customer Manager	• Review of Balanced Scorecard
	2 Partnering Values Meeting	*Customer Representatives:* • CIO • Contractor Manager *Contractor Representatives:* • Account Manager • Customer Manager	• Partnering values evaluation
Bi-Annual	1 Executive Relationship Meeting	*Customer Representatives:* • Director • CIO *Contractor Representatives:* • Managing Director • Account Manager • Customer Manager	• Future strategies • Review of overall performance
	2 Partnering Workshop	*Customer Representatives:* • Director • CIO • Contractor Manager *Contractor Representatives:* • Managing Director • Account Manager • Customer Manager	• Develop shared goals, vision, values • Develop partnering principles • Business opportunity development

Table 4.12 continued

Frequency	Meeting	Attendees	Topics
	3 Agreement Review Meeting	*Customer Representatives:* ● CIO ● Contractor Manager ● IT Manager *Contractor Representatives:* ● Account Manager ● Customer Manager ● Service Manager	● Review of audit findings ● Variations ● Review and updating of documentation ● TCO tracking ● Cost and service level benchmarking
	4 IT Strategy Meeting	*Customer Representatives:* ● CIO ● Contractor Manager ● IT Manager *Contractor Representatives:* ● Customer Manager ● Service Manager ● Technical Specialists	● IT strategic planning for the forthcoming year
Quarterly	1 SLA/Contract Review Meeting	*Customer Representatives:* ● CIO ● Contract Manager ● IT Manager *Contractor Representatives:* ● Account Manager ● Customer Manager ● Service Manager	● Review of KPIs/SFAs ● Variations ● Agreement milestone planning ● Identification of improvement opportunities, technology refresh and Server/application consolidation ● Update of asset management, equipment register, documentation and schedules ● Review of SLA against Ericsson baseline

	Attendees	Agenda
2 Technology Forum	*Customer Representatives:* • IT Manager • Business Unit Managers (where appropriate) *Contractor Representatives:* • Service Manager • Business IT and Technical Experts	• Presentation of new product releases/new technologies • Discussions relating to technology trials
3 Capacity Planning Meeting	*Customer Representatives:* • Contractor Manager • IT Manager *Contractor Representatives:* • Customer Manager • Service Manager • Capacity planning experts	• Review quarterly Capacity Planning report and recommendations
Monthly		
1 Monthly Service Review	*Customer Representatives:* • CIO • Contractor Manager • IT Manager *Contractor Representatives:* • Account Manager • Customer Manager • Service Manager	• Present all reports listed in this SLA • Review/discuss monthly reports and performance over the past month • Planning for upcoming month • Staff moves and changes • Upcoming projects
2 Pre Invoice Meeting	*Customer Representatives:* • CIO • Contractor Manager • IT Manager *Contractor Representatives:* • Account Manager • Customer Manager • Service Manager	• Review Proposed Invoice • Review SFA Report

Table 4.14 Price model approaches

Type	Description	Pro	Con	Organization's focus
Fixed-price	Lump sum fee within fixed volume range(s)	Predictable costs within the volume bands	Out of scope charges probable, can lose track of individual cost drivers	Focus on keeping demand within the fixed fee limitations and scope definitions to ensure base needs are met
Variable price	Charge per transaction unit (hours, calls, users)/schedule of rates	Cost matched to demand, easy to 'chop and change' services and volumes	Extensive demand controls as supply is effectively 'unlimited'	Focus on demand tracking and management, as price is directed related to usage
Cost plus/ Open book	Actual cost plus specified mark-up or management fee	Fill knowledge of cost dynamics	Extensive auditing and benchmarking of supplier's costs and efficiency	Focus on detailed understanding of cost drivers and supplier's efficiency, as supplier does not have an inherent motivation to improve either

the lowest bid have often had the highest overall cost as these misunderstandings come to light. In some cases, the customer has had to pay significantly more than the original estimate in order to keep the supplier solvent.

4.4 Draft the contract

The contract forms the crux of the documented governance framework for both parties. The key to a good contract is fair and comprehensive terms. The main benefit of the contract is not so much having a signed contract as it is the process it forces the parties to undergo in defining responsibilities, expectations, protocols, etc.

We have observed in recent times an alarming trend to forego investment in a prudent contract, the rationale being that the parties desire a 'partnership' based on trust and the perception that a comprehensive contract is at odds with this desire. However, this is a high-risk strategy, particularly where trust has not been earned over many years of the parties working with one another. While all potential issues can rarely be identified at the onset of a relationship, it should not preclude the development of the sound governance framework enabled by a robust contract. Inevitably, all commercial relationships will experience differing interpretations and expectations and in lieu of a contract governing rights, responsibilities and the like, the party with the strongest negotiation position at the time of the issue is likely to prevail. If the organization is not definite it will be that superior party, then it will be over-relying on the benevolence of the supplier.

There is no standard ITO contract, only standard headings. Each outsourcing arrangement has its own set of issues and dynamics. Many make the mistake of trying to 'cut and paste' previous contracts from other organizations, even for completely unrelated services. Contractual options and ITO best practices are continuously evolving. ITO contracts signed five years ago bear little resemblance to those formed today.

Case Study: a government agency

An agency responsible for the building of public infrastructure, such as roads and buildings, had determined that outsourcing of its IT infrastructure would best meet its technology and cost goals. It issued a tender, complete with the desired contract. A large portion of the contract was dedicated to the parties' rights and responsibilities over discovery of archaeological finds during the course of the contract. While such clauses are useful in road or building construction, it was readily apparent to the potential suppliers that the agency spent little effort in drafting a contract appropriate to IT services.

Compare this case study with much better practice when ICI issued an 'Invitation To Tender' together with a detailed contract for a five-year outsourcing of its datacentres. In practice, the detailed contract reflected a rare level of preparedness on the ICI team's part. This came from a thorough understanding of their in-house cost and service levels, together with a realistic expectation as to what a supplier could achieve, while still making a reasonable profit.

The majority of ITO contracts are drafted by the customer rather than using the supplier's 'standard contract' (Cullen *et al.*, 2001).

Recital

Signatories

Part 1: General Provisions
1 Interpretation
2 Definitions used in this Contract
3 Initial term of the Contract
4 Subsequent terms of the Contract
5 Governing law
6 Entire Contract and Precedence
7 Conditions precedent (due diligence, etc)
8 Severability of provisions
9 General conduct of the Contract
10 Partnering
11 Negation of employment, partnership, etc
12 Use of Customer name, logo, etc
13 Media and public relations
14 Exclusivity (or non-exclusivity)
15 Waivers
16 Guarantees, warranties and indemnities
17 Liability
18 Contractor not to encumber itself
19 Unconditional financial undertaking
20 Insurances
21 Occupational Health and Safety
22 Industry development
23 Items to be maintained in escrow
24 Assignment and novation
25 Intellectual property rights
26 Confidentiality and disclosure
27 Conflict of interest
28 Consents and transfers
29 Force majeure
30 Extraordinary events, excusable delay, extension for obligation discharge
31 Temporary suspension of services at Customer request
32 Customer step-in rights
33 Notification of disruption
34 Dispute resolution
35 Amendments and variations
36 Notices

Part 2: Service Particulars
37 Appointment of Representatives
38 General scope of Services
39 Obligations of Customer
40 Obligations of Contractor
41 Provision of services in accordance with SLA
42 Resource commitment
43 Performance guarantee
44 Applicable standards and policies
45 Contractor as Prime Contractor
46 Subcontracting
47 Contractor as agent
48 Management of third party contracts
49 Performance improvement
50 Benchmarking
51 Technology refreshment
52 Specified contractor personnel
53 Personnel image, removal, qualifications, training, etc
54 Secondments
55 Access to Customer site(s)
56 Interface requirements and access
57 Records/documentation to be maintained
58 Data ownership, integrity and security
59 Audit rights, records and access
60 Correction of defects
61 Viruses

Part 3: Financial Particulars
62 Prices/Service Fees
63 Fees for additional services outside scope
64 Gainsharing
65 Service fee adjustments for KPIs in accordance with SLA (rebates, bonuses)
66 Reimbursement of costs incurred
67 Limitation on expenditures
68 Customer offset rights for damage caused by Contractor
69 Invoicing
70 Payment
71 GST, taxes and duties

Part 4: Start-up Particulars
72 Obligations of Contractor during Start-up
73 Obligations of Customer during Start-up
74 Start-up/migration plan
75 Cutover/Acceptance certificate
76 Transfer/sale of assets
77 Transfer/secondment of staff
78 Transfer of third party licences/contracts
79 Documentation to be developed

Part 5: Termination/Disengagement Particulars
80 Termination by breach by the Customer
81 Termination by breach by the Contractor
82 Injunction restraining Contractor breach
83 Termination in absence of breach
84 Partial termination
85 Settlement of accounts/moneys recoverable
86 Transfer-back of assets / purchase of assets
87 Transfer-back of staff / offers of employment
88 Contractor service obligations during termination
89 Termination assistance by the Contractor
90 Post termination services by the Contractor
91 No representation after termination
92 Clauses surviving termination

SCHEDULES
A   Contract Details
B   Service Level Agreement (SLA)
C   Price/Service Fees
D   Service/Business//Management Plan(s)
E   Acquisitions by the Contractor (assets, staff, licences, etc)
F   Employment offer
G   Assets, licences, etc to be retained by the Customer
H   Third party contracts/licences to be managed by the Contractor
I   Unconditional financial undertaking
J   Performance Guarantee
K   Specified Subcontractors
L   Subcontractor agreements
M   Specified Personnel List
N   Confidentiality Agreement
O   Escrow Agreement
P   Partnering Charter
Q   Start-up Plan
R   Resource Plan
S   Termination Plan

Figure 4.9 Example contract outline

This is wise. Drafting the contract is invaluable in the formation of the customer's expectations and assessment of various options for each contractual topic/issue (of which we have identified over 90, see Figure 4.9). The supplier's standard contract represents the supplier's preferred version and is unlikely to reflect the needs of the customer, and even less likely to reflect the organization's desired rights.

In drafting the contract, we recommend starting out with deciding the organization's position on the standard headings. The point of starting from the headings is to decide, particular to this arrangement, what is appropriate from the plethora of options available. For each organization, the value of drafting the contract is the process it forces itself to undergo in deciding the many options and issues – not just to have a signed piece of paper. A general outline of the contract headings appears in Figure 4.9.

We do not intend to provide a comprehensive guide to contracts in this book. Each organization should seek expert commercial and legal advice to develop the particular clauses appropriate to the deal it has in mind, and structure the governing documents in such a way that the contract and SLA are easily understandable and manageable.

Case Study: a federal agency

The governing documents (contract, numerous SLAs and schedules) for one major outsourcing arrangement were so complex, poorly written and structured that it took the new Contract Manager a year to fully understand the contract, the full extent of the arrangement, and how things were to get done between the two parties well enough to be effective at his job. Then he was transferred. His replacement also lasted slightly over a year. For years there was no one at the organization who was able to discuss the arrangement without having 'rewritten' the contract in a manner they could understand.

One useful tip here, though, is to make sure that commercial, not legal, priorities dictate the final shape of the contract. Lawyers should be there to translate the agreed commercial arrangements into legally sound documents, not interfere with the commercial viability of the agreement.

Table 4.15 Missing or inadequate contract clauses

Clause	% of Respondents	Clause	% of Respondents
Performance guarantee	44%	Limitation on expenditures	9%
Benchmarking	44%	Partial termination	9%
Provision of services in accordance with SLAs	35%	Transfer-back of assets	9%
Performance improvement	35%	Conflict of interest	7%
Payment for services outside scope	35%	Transfer/sale of assets	7%
Obligations of supplier	30%	Transfer of third party licences	7%
Technology refreshment/exploitation	26%	Voluntary termination (absence of breach)	7%
Resource commitment	26%	Moneys recoverable	7%
Documentation to be maintained	22%	Escrow	6%
Documentation to be developed during start-up	22%	Assignment and novation	6%
Partnering	20%	Force majeure	6%
Subcontracting	20%	Records, access and audit rights	6%
Applicable standards and policies	20%	Viruses	6%
Gainsharing	20%	Service fees	6%
Obligations of supplier during start-up	20%	Invoicing	6%
Guarantees, warranties and indemnities	19%	Transfer/secondment of staff	6%
Liability cap	17%	Termination by breach by the supplier	6%
Management of third party contract(s)	17%	Service obligations during termination	6%
Migration/handover plan	17%	Initial contract term	4%
Obligations of customer during start-up	17%	Subsequent terms of the contract	4%
Intellectual property rights	15%	Confidentiality and disclosure	4%
Service fee adjustments	15%	Year 2000 compliance	4%
Renegotiation	13%	Transfer of third party contracts	4%
Industry development	13%	Termination by breach by the customer	4%
Transfer-back of staff	13%	Termination assistance required	4%
Dispute resolution	11%	Post termination services required	4%
Service fee variations	11%	Recital	2%
Exclusivity	9%	Unconditional financial undertaking	2%
Amendments and variations	9%	Supplier as prime contractor	2%
Extension of time for excusable delay	9%	Supplier as agent on customer behalf	2%
Obligations of customer	9%	Consents and transfers	2%
Specified supplier personnel	9%	Appointment of representatives	2%
Secondments	9%	Insurances	0%
Service resource plan	9%	Reimbursement of costs incurred	0%
Data ownership and security	9%	Payment	0%

Source: Cullen *et al.* (2001), 54 respondents

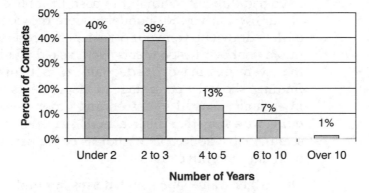

Length of Initial Contract Term

Source: Cullen et al (2001) 90 contracts

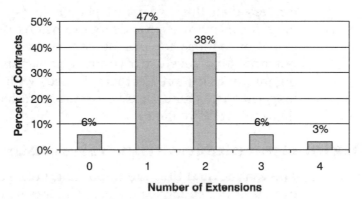

Times Contract can be Extended

Source: Cullen et al (2001) 70 contracts

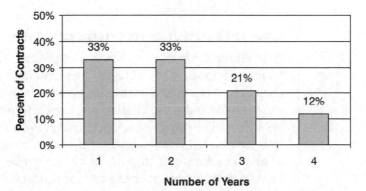

Length of Extensions

Figure 4.10
Contract length and
extension options

Source: Cullen et al (2001) 32 contracts

It may be useful to know which contractual topics organizations have had difficulty with in the past. In Table 4.15 are the results of our own survey. Respondents were provided with a contract outline drawn up from our own experience as to what should go into a contract. Respondents were asked to identify all clauses that were missing or inadequate in their own contracts. The findings show the percentage of respondents with inadequacies in each area, sorted in descending order. Personally, we find it quite worrying that such a high percentage of organizations seem to have noticeable weakness in the performance measurement and incentive areas.

Of further value are some norms around the length of the contract and extensions. Rather than have the five- to seven-year contracts of the last decade, contracts are now being broken into manageable timeframes which have short initial terms and options for extensions. In recent times, the initial term has been for less than three years, as shown in Figure 4.10. The vast majority of contracts provide for extensions, typically one or two extension options for one or two years each. This gives the potential for a seven-year contract, rather than locking it. Few organizations can predict their IT needs with any certainty over long lengths of time, thus it is prudent to have flexibility over the contract continuance.

4.5 Model the relationship behaviour

The contract and SLA are important, but relatively superficial, drivers of day-to-day behaviour. The true behaviour-drivers are the underlying values and behaviour adopted by the individual parties and the people involved in the agreement. However, poor contracts can make for poor relationships, if you are not careful.

Case Study: a manufacturer

One client agreed to a clause stipulating that 'all costs of transfer of software licensing agreements will be borne by the client'. The first 30 transfers cost relatively little, but the next ten virtually eliminated the cost savings from the five-year deal. The supplier argued that it was a standard clause that he needed in the contract if it was to make any money at all. The client felt that he had been tricked. The two sides beat each other up over every ambiguous clause they could find for the rest of the contract's duration.

Relationship Values Charter

Introduction

The Customer has identified that if outsourcing is to work effectively, the Contractor must become an integral part of the organisation and a true enabler. Both Parties must work towards a type of 'partnering relationship'.

However, the Parties agree that their legal relationship must always be governed by the Contract. Nevertheless, the Parties have identified that a process needs to be implemented to enable both Parties to work effectively without the Contract being relied on in every instance.

To achieve this, the Parties wish to set out their common goals that are to operate during the course of their relationship in this 'Charter of Values' and use it as a process for review and high-level measurement.

The Values

Value	Description
1 Service Expectations	We do not desire to apply Service Fee Adjustments. The Services will be of a consistent high standard, comparable to market standards, and the End Users will be delighted.
2 Financial	We will achieve our financial goals: • Customer – to reduce cost over time and have market competitive pricing at all times • Contractor – to have reasonable profits.
3 Communication	We will communicate frequently, openly and honestly with each other.
4 Meet Needs	We will be both proactive and reactive to each other's needs. We will provide each other time and management focus.
5 Continuous Improvement	We will constantly search for better ways of doing things.
6 Conflict	We recognise conflict as natural and will focus on solving the problem, not apportioning blame. We will resolve conflict at the lowest level appropriate.
7 Fairness	We will be fair to all parties.
8 External Relations	We will project a united front and will not discuss sensitive issues with individuals outside of the relationship.
9 Industry Model	We desire our relationship to be seen as an industry model.
10 Enjoyment	We enjoy working together and respect one another.
11 Added Value	We will both derive more value from our relationship than just the exchange of money for services.
12 Work Seamlessly	The IT services value chain will appear seamless to the End User.
13 Technology Leadership	We will have recognised technology leadership in the provision of the Services.

Figure 4.11 Example relationship values charter (continued overleaf)

Scoring the Values

The parties agree to implement and review their relationship according to this Charter by each scoring their perception of their relationship according to the following table on at least a quarterly basis:

Category	1 Unacceptable	2 We are worried	3 Just motoring	4 Looking good	5 Absolutely delighted
1 Service Expectations					
2 Financial					
3 Communication					
4 Meet Needs					
5 Creative Solutions					
6 Conflict					
7 Fairness					
8 External Relations					
9 Industry Model					
10 Enjoyment					
11 Added Value					
12 Works Seamlessly					
13 Technology Leadership					

Having evaluated and scored their relationship, each party will provide the other with:

- Justification of each score given
- Identify why and improvements required
- Proposed solution

Figure 4.11 continued

By contrast, mature outsourcing organizations have adopted a form of agreement, typically called a 'Relationship Values Charter' with relation to the model behaviour they wish demonstrated during the course of the relationship (see Figure 4.11). Often this is a schedule to the contract, with a subjective evaluation conducted by both parties on at least an annual basis. Modelling the desired behaviours at this stage in the process is valuable as it can significantly contribute to the selection of the supplier organization that best demonstrates it lives these values, particularly as getting the right value and culture between the parties has proved to be one of the most difficult aspects of an outsourcing agreement (Cullen *et al.*, 2001).

4.6 Plan the future management

The use of outsourcing does not imply less effort in managing IT, only a different emphasis. For example, the top IT manager will need to concentrate more on direction, strategy and implementation than with routine service delivery and staff management. Table 4.16 provides a brief overview of the impact of ITO on general IT management activities.

Any organization is in a superior position if it develops the future IT organization and contract/supplier management strategy early. The time to decide what needs to be done and by whom is not after the deal has been signed and everyone has either left or transferred to the supplier. It is tempting to wait and try to 'make a go of it', but this approach assumes a level of effortlessness regarding ITO management that rarely exists. This fatal flaw has left some organizations with out-of-control costs, high IT personnel turnover, inadequate supplier monitoring and poor IT planning.

Case Study: an insurance company

A state-based insurance company had entered into a 'strategic partnership' with an IT organization. The board, believing that the supplier was now its official IT department and would act accordingly, saw no need to retain any IT capability. Accordingly, it outsourced the entirety of its IT people, processes, technology and strategy to the supplier. After the transition was completed, the soon-to-be-exiting CIO realized that no thinking had taken place regarding managing the supplier, let alone managing the utilization of

IT in the company. He commissioned a study to determine what prudent management should be in place and was startled with the level of basic management required alone. He proposed the resultant IT and contract management strategy to the board, but was over-ruled. The board put the supplier in charge of its own contract instead. Five years later, IT strategy was non-existent and IT costs were demonstrably higher than the market. The organization has started to rebuild its IT organization, beginning with the hiring of a CIO.

Table 4.16 ITO impact on IT management activities

Activity	Impact
Approving	The need to appropriately authorize plans, costs, recommendations, and actions and sign off on deliverables increases. Rarely will a supplier begin work without appropriate approvals or allow a customer organization not to sign off acceptance of a deliverable
Auditing	Auditing (compliance, validation and value for money) is generally more extensive and frequent because of these underlying conditions: • the organization's accountability remains static; • autocratic control and physical proximity are absent; and • the introduction of profit as a key motivation by the external supplier
Evaluating	The need to appropriately evaluate plans, costs, recommendations, actions and deliverables becomes greater because of the cost of rework
Negotiating	Needs and requirements that require changes will need to be negotiated and have a cost impact, whereas under insourcing employees could be told what to do. In most ITO contracts, other than a straight contract labour agreement, the customer organization is not allowed to direct the workforce of the supplier
Performing	Performance of activities outsourced is the domain of the supplier, although the organization must direct and contribute to those services. Accountability for the ultimate service outcome always ends with the organization as, at the end of the day, the supplier is merely an agent for the organization
Planning	Planning becomes absolutely critical in outsourced environments. It is the familiar 'garbage in – garbage out' paradigm, however the garbage will cost more
Staying informed	The organization must have information equal to the supplier to be able to effectively evaluate all aspects of the services. Furthermore, it must stay informed of any events that may affect the relationship, externally and within the supplier. Accordingly, the breadth of the information requirements of the retained IT organization actual increase

How the organization decides to structure its responsibilities will impact on all future processes in the outsourcing lifecycle. It will impact on how services are defined, the bids it may get from the suppliers, and the total cost for the business case and the success of the deal in the long run.

The strategies that we recommend are developed at this stage are the two interdependent ones below:

- Retained organization strategy.
- Contract management strategy.

Refer to the seventh Building Block – 'Get the results: manage the ITO' for the detailed discussion on contract and relationship management.

4.6.1 Retained organization strategy

The retained organization represents what it is that is necessary to remain in the organization in order to manage the contract, perform the out of scope work processes, and manage any interfaces within the organization, between the organization and the supplier, and between both parties with third parties.

A retained organization strategy documents the:

1 retained services, functions and work processes that will continue to be performed by the organization;
2 revised organization structure incorporating all interfaces internal and external to the organization;
3 roles and responsibilities of the retained organization;
4 costs for the retained organization, including investment in new skills.

We have observed that many organizations have cut too deep into their IT organization after outsourcing. At face value, not having duplicate technical skill sets between the two parties appears to be a rational decision, and it is for many skill sets. However, where the function:

- has a considerable impact on the business and is a primary enabler of business initiatives (i.e. IT strategy);
- requires an intimate knowledge of the organization and is required to obtain best value from that skill for it to be effective (i.e. business analysis); or

1 Structure and Accountabilities
   1.1 Retained Organization
   1.2 Contract Management Network

2 Planned High Level Flowcharts
   2.1 Work Processes
   2.2 Information Flows

3 Contract Management Network Activities
   3.1 Reporting and Monitoring
      3.1.1 Costs
      3.1.2 Service
      3.1.3 Strategic Objectives
   3.2 Payments
      3.2.1 Invoice Acceptance
      3.2.2 Service Fee Adjustments (penalties & rewards)
   3.3 Contract Control
      3.3.1 Documentation and Record keeping
      3.3.2 Approvals & Signoffs
      3.3.3 Contract & SLA Variations
      3.3.4 Risk Management
      3.3.5 Problem/Issue Identification
      3.3.6 Dispute Resolution
      3.3.7 Service Continuity Plan
      3.3.8 End of Contract
   3.4 Audits
      3.4.1 Costs
      3.4.2 Service Quality and Control
      3.4.3 Contract Compliance
   3.5 KPI Reporting Reviews
      3.5.1 Of Service Provider
      3.5.2 Internal Effectiveness and Efficiency
   3.6 Planning & Forecasting
      3.6.1 Demand and Capacity Requirements
      3.6.2 Changes to Requirements and Business Needs
      3.6.3 Continuous Improvement
      3.6.4 MACs (Moves, Additions, and Changes) to Services
   3.7 Meetings
      3.7.1 Operational
      3.7.2 Review
      3.7.3 Strategic Planning

4 Key Protocols Between the Parties
   4.1 Communication
   4.2 Authorizations/Approvals
   4.3 Variations
   4.4 Requests

5 Key Dates & Milestones
   5.1 High Level Timetable
   5.2 Organizational Milestones
   5.3 Service Provider Milestones
   5.4 Contract Management Unit Milestones

Attachment - Job Descriptions

Figure 4.12 Contract management strategy outline

- has many alternative solutions and price options that require ongoing decisions to be made in the organization's best interest (i.e. configuration, procurement),

an organization is rarely well served by a supplier performing those functions.

4.6.2 Contract management strategy

Today's contract managers have greater responsibility because the nature of contracting has changed. Current contracts can:

- have a large scope of services provided;
- have a great impact on customers;
- have more responsibility assumed by the supplier;
- often involve the transfer of assets and staff;
- employ a 'partnering' style of relationship; and
- involve complex relationships between prime- and subcontractors and between other third party suppliers.

The changing nature of contracting means that the managing responsibility transcends the traditional, more administrative role. To manage today's contracts, a direct role must be played at a strategic and operational level to ensure value for money is achieved and risks are minimized.

The minimum the organization may want to consider to do at this stage is to develop the contract management strategy. Figure 4.12 provides a contract management strategy outline that can guide planning.

This chapter will have given the reader a real sense of how much preparatory work needs to be done if an organization is to give itself a realistic chance of leveraging outsourcing successfully. But so far we have hardly even considered how you go about selecting suppliers, and negotiating with the service provider of your choice. These are the themes of the next building block.

Part Two

Engage Phase

5

The fifth building block – commercial mating: select the supplier(s)

Architect				Engage		Govern	
Discard myths	Prepare strategies	Target services	Design future	Select supplier(s)	Make transition	Manage the ITO	Reconsider options

Determining what supplier(s) the organization is going to live with and depend upon for many years is akin to an arranged marriage, albeit one in which the organization has sole discretion. A vigilant selection process will deliver the best supplier against the organization's established needs. From then on, it is up to the parties to govern themselves appropriately.

A competitive process is the most common selection technique and most organizations employ a tender to select their ITO suppliers. Such an approach provides pressure on suppliers to deliver best value for money against their industry peers, exposes the organization to a variety of capabilities and potential solutions, and allows an informed selection decision to evolve and mature.

Of course, entering into direct negotiation is an alternative approach for organizations in the appropriate position. An organization considering this approach is in the best position to successfully execute this strategy if the following characteristics are present:

- Only one supplier is suitable – there is no benefit in evaluating alternative suppliers.
- The organization is an informed buyer – knows what is a reasonable market price and knows industry norms regarding service definitions, technology, KPIs, etc. There is no need to employ competitive pressure to get the best deal.
- The organization knows exactly what it wants, and can quickly draw up an effective contract, SLA and price model.

Table 5.1 Selection strategy checklist

---

1 How will we ensure this is a successful selection process?
- What are the critical success factors of this process?
- What are the risks and barriers that can prevent us achieving these critical success factors? How can we mitigate them?
- What assumptions must we make before proceeding?

2 What will be our approach to the market?
- Should we use a single stage or multi-stage approach? Do we want to scan the market with an RFI? Shortlist via an EOI? Use a BAFO for competitive negotiation?
- Will this be an open (publicly advertised) or closed (invitation only) selection process? If open, how do we want to advertise and distribute the tender? If closed, how do we determine which suppliers should be invited to respond?
- Do we want a 'two envelope' response separating price from the other information requirements?

3 What information will we provide to the bidders?
- Will we draft the contract and SLAs as part of the market package?
- What operational diagrams, data and statistics will we provide? Covering what time period(s)?
- What future strategies and plans will we provide?
- Will we disclose our evaluation criteria? Will we disclose the weightings?
- Will we let the bidders know who else is bidding?

4 How will we facilitate the bids to get the best possible responses?
- What should we communicate to the market and when?
- How should we brief the market? Will we have collective or individual briefings?
- Do we want *pro forma* responses to make evaluation easier?
- How will we get the bidders familiar with our operations? Will we have site visits? A data room? Allow interviews of key stakeholders?
- How will we run the questions and answers? Will all Q&A be distributed to the bidders?

5 How will we ensure that this selection process is defensible?
- What are the 'ground rules' to ensure probity throughout this selection process?
- How will we declare and manage potential conflicts of interest?
- Do we need a probity adviser and/or a probity auditor? If so, what roles will they play and when?
- Will we have an independent probity review performed and when will this occur?

6 How will we ensure we pick the right supplier?
- What criteria and scoring techniques will we use?
- What will be our techniques to evaluate suppliers besides the bid itself? Interviews? Site visits? Customer references? Due diligence?
- Does the evaluation team have the right mix of strategic, technical, commercial and financial evaluators?
- Are the team members able to commit to the project?
- What type of education does the team require before commencing evaluation?
- Do we want a secure evaluation room or will we distribute the bids to the team?
- Who has final approval of the team's recommendation?

7 How will we inform bidders of their success or otherwise?
- Will we announce the preferred supplier or wait until the deal is signed?
- How will we notify unsuccessful bidders and when?
- Will we offer a debrief to unsuccessful bidders? Who must be present?

- Speed is more important than cost, exploring alternative solutions or making comparisons. But be careful here not to throw away any advantage from speed through poor preparation and ultimately self-defeating decisions.
- The organization is an experienced outsourcing manager – it can expertly manage the supplier and the arrangement.

For everyone else, however, a competitive process is the most appropriate. In their research on proven practices, Lacity and Willcocks (2001) found non-competed bids having a very mixed track record. Table 5.1 provides a checklist designed to help organizations prepare their selection strategy. The checklist reflects the many questions and tasks that naturally arise in the process of selecting a supplier.

5.1 Selection is *not* the first block – ensure the ITO foundation has been laid

We now enter the Engage Phase. This is a critical point in the ITO lifecycle, where the costs of the lifecycle project can begin to escalate. Any shortcuts taken and any parts of the four Architect Phase building blocks left out before this point will have an adverse impact on the success of the ITO arrangement. Without architecting, buildings are not safe. In the same way the Architect Phase provides vital design and foundation blocks. Beginning the lifecycle at the Engage Phase is the equivalent of starting to build a house before designing the plans and hoping it will all come together. In Figure 5.1, we trace the different paths, in terms of effort and cost, of different levels of client thoroughness and activity across the first four building blocks. In the 'flawed path', you can also see the most typical characteristics of poor practice and their later consequences.

Unfortunately for many organizations, the selection stage was the starting point for them and very limited components, if any, of the Architect Phase (the first four building blocks) were conducted. Some have invested heavily in a comprehensive tender and had inadequate and/or limited response, necessitating a complete rethink of the sourcing strategy and approach because of a number of factors including:

- being unaware of the market conditions – more attractive tenders/opportunities out in the market had consumed the resources of the suppliers;

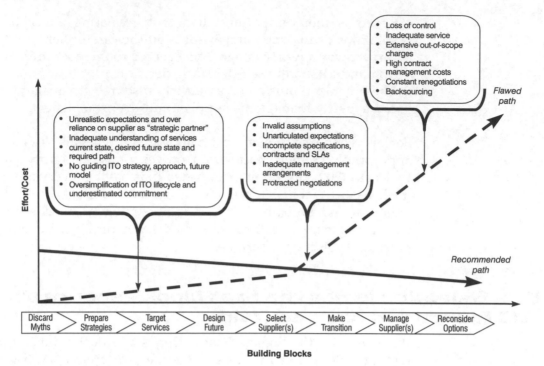

Figure 5.1 Lifecycle cost escalation

- written an adversarial contract – with the maturity of the market and achievement of economies, suppliers are more reluctant to 'buy' adversarial customers and corresponding risks unless price premiums are part of the arrangement;
- assuming everyone would want their business – suppliers are maturing in their 'bid/no bid' criteria, and are more likely to target desired customers rather than opportunistically respond to customers not on the desired list. Part of the battle can involve convincing the market that the organization intends to contract the service. Suppliers have indicated to us that they believe only 20% of approaches to them are genuine.
- not providing a perceived level playing field – particularly where there is an incumbent supplier or the in-house service organization is also competing in some manner; or
- being too vague as to the nature of the expectations – including what services are being considered for outsourcing and the current/future state of those services, what type of capabilities are being sought, price expectations and model, the plan for the full lifecycle, etc, resulting in a high cost for the supplier to ascertain the missing information or the need to attach such a risk premium that it removes any cost advantage the supplier may have been able to offer.

The selection stage and the prior Architect Phase are also where the organization is in its greatest position of influence. Once a contract has been awarded, the organization's bargaining power erodes because much competitive tension has been removed. Furthermore, once a preferred supplier is known, all variations to any aspect of the proposed arrangement require negotiation, and by that time many organizations are under time and cost constraints to execute and transition-in the arrangement. Lastly, once an agreement is in place, an organization will have few cost effective options compared to the pre-govern phases and is, in effect, under a quasi-monopolistic supply situation.

Figure 5.2 shows how bargaining power can operate under our approach. Should an organization enter the lifecycle without having built the best possible bargaining power prior to the Engage Phase, the bargaining power it has will often never exceed the moderate to low levels with commensurate degradation in all subsequent building blocks.

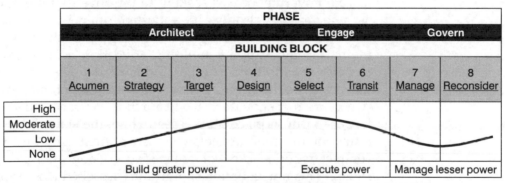

Figure 5.2 Customer bargaining power in the lifecycle

Prior to embarking on the selection process, the organization should have conducted the following processes at a minimum. Check that you have done so.

- Collected all the information necessary to be an informed buyer – adequate knowledge of the potential suppliers, market conditions, ITO best practice, etc.
- Decided its preferred approach to the entire outsourcing lifecycle and determined strategic preferences.
- Targeted the services to be considered for outsourcing, including the preparation of full profiles (service, cost,

balance sheet, staff, commercial relationships, stakeholders and service management).

- Designed, to the extent possible, the future arrangement including the contract, SLA and retained organization, including the contract management function.
- Clarified the impact of all relevant issues that may not be certain during the life of the contract and that may affect the services demand. Examples include corporate changes (for example, company restructuring, business unit disposals, mergers/acquisitions), new system implementations or retirements and IT infrastructure refreshment. The organization should separate out all issues it is certain of, and all those that there is a degree of uncertainty. Suppliers are usually eager to help potential customers with the uncertain aspects and available alternatives.

Case Study: a state government

A state government was seeking to improve its reputation as a technology leader. It requested offers for an outsourcing contract covering its technology infrastructure in return for the supplier building education and research facilities in addition to other industry development initiatives. Once the winning offer was awarded, it took nearly two years to negotiate the outsourcing contract and even longer to put in place SLAs. Meanwhile, the state of the IT infrastructure requirements changed dramatically and the contract required a major renegotiation soon after it was signed. This renegotiation significantly lessened the supplier's scope of work and profits, thus the industry development proposal was likewise significantly curtailed. Both parties continue to invest considerable effort into creating a reasonable outcome for all concerned.

5.2 Gating and refining via staged competitive tendering

We generally recommend that a multi-staged tendering approach be taken, unless the organization is effectively in the same situation as those that could adopt the direct negotiation approach. That is, the organization is an informed buyer, knows exactly what it wants, and is an experienced outsourcing manager. Generally, however, we find that organizations do benefit from the introduction of competition into the process.

Some organizations have believed that it is most efficient to attempt to go to the market once, rather than multiple times, but these have learnt that this belief often comes from inexperienced IT management or procurement specialists who over-simplify the engagement process of an ITO arrangement.

The selection of suppliers via a competitive tendering process can involve any number of stages. The appropriate utilization of each stage depends upon the:

- organization's knowledge of the market – it may be on a learning curve and thus needing a more exploratory process;
- stability of the market offerings – short product/service method lifecycles may require the organization to update knowledge and scan offerings;
- degree of influx of new entrants – that can change market dynamics and present one-off opportunities for the organization;
- number of potential suppliers – that may require culling for a cost-effective evaluation process;
- degree to which the organization knows what it wants – it may want to explore options and alternatives; or
- completeness and competitiveness of the bids in the preceding stages – additional stages may be required or unnecessary stages removed depending upon the responses.

The typical tender stages you may choose to embark upon, together with indicative supplier response periods, are shown in Table 5.2.

A multi-stage tendering process functions primarily to filter the potential pool of suppliers with the least effort at each stage, leaving the organization with a manageable number of potentially voluminous bids to conduct its detailed evaluation.

It is important to concentrate effort here for all concerned, not least to keep costs down. Bid costs can be significant, and indeed may be a significant inhibitor for some suppliers, where they feel they might not be the client's first choice. To give some indications, we have found that bid costs can fall between 0.4% and 2.5% of total outsourcing costs. Interestingly, in 2003 the UK Inland Revenue made available some £8 million to suppliers to attract enough bidders.

Table 5.2 Typical tender stages

Stage		When to use the stage	What to seek from suppliers	What to provide to suppliers	Indicative supplier response period
ROI	Registration of Interest	• To gain familiarity with the market • To determine who may be interested in bidding • To shortlist for next stage	• General business data (services, size, customers, etc) • High level experience in scope	• Requirements on type of supplier appropriate to register (capabilities, geographic scope, etc)	1–2 weeks
RFI	Request for Information	• To assess total market capability • Gather detailed information about potential bidders • To shortlist for next stage	• Detailed business data and viability information • Detailed experience relevant to scope	• Capabilities sought • Service scope • Geographic scope • Resources	2–3 weeks
EOI	Expression of Interest	• To explore options specific to the requirements • To obtain indicative prices • To shortlist for next stage	• Specific experience and results achieved relevant to scope • Indicative price • Approach options specific to this arrangement • Potential subcontractors • References	• Specific requirements • Indicative price model	3–4 weeks
RFT/ RFP/ RFO/ RFQ	Request for Tender, Proposal, Offer or Quotation	• When the requirements are explicit • To select the preferred contractor(s)	• Detailed service approach – plans, staff, assets, subcontractors, etc • References • Detailed items to negotiate from the draft agreement • Detailed and firm pricing	• Draft Contract • Draft SLA • Draft price model	4–8 weeks
BAFO	Best and Final Offer	• When a few bidders are neck-and-neck • To conduct final negotiations under competitive tension	• All aspects of final bid	• Final contract and SLA • Final price model	2–3 weeks

All parties tend to gain from the necessary preparatory work and gating process. Benefits include:

- Allows for pre-qualification and the progressive shortlisting of tenders.
- Suppliers with a slim chance of winning are spared the cost and time of preparing a full tender and the evaluation team spared the effort of conducting a detailed evaluation of bids without realistic prospects.
- Incentivizes the market to participant – full 'one hit' tenders often act as a disincentive to bid due to the high cost of bidding coupled with the lower probability of winning a contract.
- There is relatively less expensive cost of progressively responding – with the full tender investment to be incurred only if the supplier has a relatively equal or greater probability of winning.
- Allows for withdrawal from the process, if required, before significant investment is made by the organization.
- Allows exploration of service options and evolution of service requirements as stages progress.

5.3 Getting the right perspectives – the evaluation team

The evaluation team exists to:

- develop the evaluation strategy and criteria for evaluating bids;
- evaluate bids in accordance with the evaluation strategy and prepare the business case;
- determine the nature of and perform due diligence (technical, financial, customer and contractual); and
- provide recommendations to the organization based on their assessment of the preferred bid.

The individuals involved in the evaluation are paramount to selecting the most appropriate supplier. It is their unique experiences, perceptions and values that drive the assessment. If they choose poorly, for whatever reason, it could be years before the organization can unwind the outcome.

Accordingly, as we have observed in an earlier chapter, it is critical to long-term success of the outsourcing arrangement to have a broad, cross-functional team comprising at this stage the following skill sets or perspectives as required:

- Customer – expert in the customer needs and perceptions.
- Service – expert in the services in scope and those services out of scope that will have interdependence on the tendered services.
- Technical – expert in the technology options and integration requirements.
- Organizational management – expert in the business and politics of the organization.
- Contract management – expert in managing outsourcing arrangements and will be managing the contract if awarded.
- Supplier selection or purchasing – expert in the procurement process and probity.
- Legal – expert in ITO contracts.
- Financial – expert in pricing models, sensitivity analysis, accounting and due diligence.
- Human resources – expert in staff transfers, redundancies and general HRM.
- Independent advisers – experts in outsourcing, best practice, the industry and market, commercial deals.

5.4 Determining the decisive factors – the criteria

It is critical for the effectiveness of the entire competitive process for the organization to decide how it will evaluate bids before issuing a request to bidders, and prior to drafting the request in the first place. If the organization issues a request from suppliers (be it a request for information, tender, final offer) before deciding how to evaluate it, the probability of a faulty request increases dramatically. Organizations who have waited until the information is received to determine how to evaluate it have:

- omitted critical data, and thus had unexpectedly varying responses based on the assumptions made by each bidder;
- not requested appropriate information to form part of the response, and thus needed to continually ask for further information and setback the timeline;
- over emphasized non-critical areas, and accordingly had responses that concentrated on the non-critical aspects of their bid; and

- had an unstructured request hindering an efficient response by the bidders, and thus had an inefficient evaluation by the evaluation team.

The following experience of a bank gives you some idea of the sort of problems that can arise here.

Case Study: a bank

A bank issued a voluminous expression of interest (EOI) in an open tender process, giving primarily data about its operations, but also requiring information from the interested suppliers. After receiving 14 widely variant responses, it determined that it could only meet its evaluation deadline by having a structured evaluation methodology. This was particularly necessary because the evaluation team of 11 IT personnel didn't have experience in assessing outsourcing bids.

At the close of the methodology workshop convened to develop the evaluation criteria, it was discovered that only 30% of the information required by the team to enable it to determine a reasonable shortlist was actually requested in the EOI. Accordingly, no decision was made. Rather than suffer any credibility loss with the market, all 14 suppliers that responded were invited to the RFQ phase. This added two months to the evaluation period and an extra $200 000 to the project budget without having made any progress in being able to choose a supplier. Not to mention the cost to the 14 suppliers, of which 13 invested in the extensive RFQ process and lost.

Where the bid price is the sole criterion, the evaluation process is relatively straightforward. However, where 'value for money' is the key criterion, the tender evaluation becomes more complex. Value is often intangible and subject to the perceptions of the valuer, thus each organization must develop a way of assessing the value each supplier and their bid offers in terms of unquantifiable attributes. These include qualities such as experience in the services, knowledge of the specialist areas, range of skills and technology, flexibility, responsiveness and demonstrated continuous improvement.

There are three types of selection criteria:

1 Mandatory – first gate in which the bidders must pass to be considered further.
2 Qualitative – the 'value' part of the value for money equation.
3 Cost – the 'money' part of the value for money equation

Mandatory criteria are those 'drop dead' criteria that represent the first gate the bidders need to go through to be considered further. Typically these are of such importance that it does not matter how good they are or how low the price is if such criteria are not met. Mandatory criteria can be either binary (yes or no – the supplier meets them or it does not), or a minimum score (if a bidder does not meet the minimum score in any one mandatory criterion, it is disqualified).

Examples of mandatory criteria used in practice are:

● quality accreditation (e.g. ISO);
● existing service locations in the organization's required geographical scope;
● financial viability; and/or
● full response (i.e. no partial bids for selective services).

Bids that pass the mandatory criteria then progress to the next stage of evaluation – the detailed qualitative criteria. These criteria represent the array of non-price attributes the supplier is

Figure 5.3
Required supplier capabilities

offering. There has been little research on required ITO supplier capabilities, but our own experience is summarized in Figure 5.3, which suggests that every supplier can be judged against ten vital capabilities.

The degree to which each organization views these capabilities as important and the manner in which each interprets these capabilities varies of course, which is why we provide no standard evaluation criteria and/or relative weighting. Like an ITO contract, there are only standard headings (see Table 5.3), and each organization must construct their own distinctive listing to best suit the organization's purposes.

It is very common that qualitative criteria are allocated weights according to their relative importance by the evaluation team.

Table 5.3 Qualitative criteria list

Criteria component	Description
General capability	These criteria reflect the general nature of the supplier including its service and geographic portfolio, strength of its business and its ability to take on the arrangement proposed
Specific experience	These criteria reflect the detailed skill of the supplier covering the proposed arrangement including services, industry and the arrangement itself
Technical approach	These criteria reflect the detailed technical solutions proposed by the supplier and its integration, flexibility and innovation
Staffing approach	These criteria reflect the detailed staffing solutions proposed by the supplier including structure, qualifications and sustainability (depth, contingency arrangements, retention strategies, etc.)
Risk management approach	These criteria reflect the detailed risk minimization solutions proposed by the supplier including the degree of compliance with the contract/SLA, approach to risk/reward sharing, variations, disputes and disengagement
Transition approach	These criteria reflect the detailed mobilization solutions proposed by the supplier including the comprehensive plan and respective roles of the parties, take-up of staff and assets, and minimization of disruption to operations
Account management approach	These criteria reflect the detailed relationship management solutions proposed by the supplier including 'partnering', reporting, and continuous improvement
Financial approach	These criteria reflect the detailed financial solutions proposed by the supplier (excluding price) including the pricing structure and sensitivity, cost reduction approach and 'incentives'

The value of conducting a weighting of the criteria is not so much in the final weights, although that and price do determine the ultimately successful supplier. Rather, it is the process and debate that occurs to arrive at the criteria and corresponding weights that provides the real value. For this reason, a diverse evaluation team has a greater probability of developing a robust

Table 5.4 Example weighted qualitative criteria

Evaluation criteria	Subcriteria Weighting	Overall value
1. General Service Provider Capability		
1.1. Services portfolio and segment market share	10%	1.5%
1.2. Human resources approach	15%	2.3%
1.3. Financial strength and viability	30%	4.5%
1.4. Geographic scope	15%	2.3%
1.5. Business strategies	5%	0.8%
1.6. Over-reliance on key customer(s)/subcontractor(s)	5%	0.8%
1.7. Ability to add value to the organization	10%	1.5%
1.8. Capacity to undertake the business	10%	1.5%
Total percentage for Service Provider Capability	**100%**	**15.0%**
2. Service Provider Specific Experience		
2.1. Experience and coverage regarding in scope services	25%	7.5%
2.2. Demonstrated experience in similar arrangements	10%	3.0%
2.3. Demonstrated experience in similar industry	10%	3.0%
2.4. Demonstrated experience in similar organizations	5%	1.5%
2.5. Major achievements on behalf of customers	5%	1.5%
2.6. Breadth and depth of potential additional services desired	5%	1.5%
2.7. Customer reference checks	30%	9.0%
2.8. Experience as a Prime Contractor (if applicable)	10%	3.0%
Total percentage for Service Provider Experience	**100%**	**30.0%**
3. Technical Approach		
3.1. Technical suitability of proposed solution	35%	7.0%
3.2. Integration approach	25%	5.0%
3.3. Technology refresh solution	10%	2.0%
3.4. Capacity to meet fluctuation in demand/flexibility	15%	3.0%
3.5. Conformance to relevant standards	5%	1.0%
3.6. Proposed innovation	10%	2.0%
Total percentage for Technical Approach	**100%**	**20.0%**
4. Staffing Approach		
4.1. Proposed operational structure including subcontractors	25%	3.8%
4.2. Qualifications and experience of proposed team	35%	5.3%
4.3. Turnover, retention and replacement strategy	20%	3.0%
4.4. Key Personnel interviews	20%	3.0%
Total percentage for Staffing Approach	**100%**	**15.0%**

selection process. A wide range of experiences and values will facilitate the debate on what is most important for the particular ITO arrangement and why.

To get you started, an example of a weighted evaluation criteria approach is shown in Table 5.4.

Table 5.4 continued

Evaluation criteria	Subcriteria Weighting	Overall value
5. Risk Management Approach		
5.1. Proposed changes to the Contract and Service Level Agreement	30%	3.0%
5.2. Shared risk/reward approach	10%	1.0%
5.3. Service continuity plan and disaster recovery arrangements	15%	1.5%
5.4. Variation approach	10%	1.0%
5.5. Dispute resolution	5%	0.5%
5.6. Disengagement/termination approach	30%	3.0%
Total percentage for Risk Management Approach Subcriteria	100%	10.0%
6. Transition Approach		
6.1. Mobilization strategy	15%	1.5%
6.2. Transition plan and timetable	30%	3.0%
6.3. Staff transfer opportunities (if applicable)	15%	1.5%
6.4. Asset purchase approach (if applicable)	10%	1.0%
6.5. Roles proposed over both parties and degree of responsibility taken	20%	2.0%
6.6. Disruption minimization	10%	1.0%
Total percentage for Transition Approach Subcriteria	100%	10.0%
7. Account Management Approach		
7.1. Account management structure and personnel	15%	2.3%
7.2. Partnering relationship approach	20%	3.0%
7.3. Reporting and billing systems	10%	1.5%
7.4. Service improvement agenda	20%	3.0%
7.5. Customer satisfaction assessment approach	10%	1.5%
7.6. Knowledge transfer techniques	5%	0.8%
7.7. Benchmarking approach	20%	3.0%
Total percentage for all Account Management Subcriteria	100%	15.0%
8. Financial Approach Assessment		
8.1. Pricing structure	10%	1.5%
8.2. Cost reduction approach	30%	4.5%
8.3. Price sensitivity	30%	4.5%
8.4. Penalty/reward structure	10%	1.5%
8.5. Termination changes	20%	3.0%
Total percentage for all Financial Assessment Subcriteria	100%	15.0%
Total percentage for all criteria (1–8)		100.0%

In a multi-staged tender, some criteria may get recycled, albeit with different weights, and carried forward to the next stage and some may drop off as unnecessary for the advanced stages.

Once the criteria and their relative importance are developed, the process of identifying the information you need from potential bidders, appropriate to the stage of the competitive process, can begin. As we have stated earlier, it is the most efficient use of time and intellect to develop the information requirements after determining what criteria will be driving the selection process. It's a win–win outcome. The supplier does not waste time on low-priority items and the task of evaluation is simplified.

5.5 Exhibiting fairness – probity

A key matter to document in the selection strategy is about the issue of probity. Probity is concerned with providing bidders, and the wider community, with confidence in the integrity and fairness of the process. This encourages a wider field of bids and a greater investment in the process by the bidders. The lack of probity can jeopardize not only the selection being undertaken, but future opportunities as well.

Potential bidders need to be confident that they will be treated professionally, that no preference will be given to any bidder and that there is information parity with all bidders. Probity failures need only to be *perceived* to cause the organization difficulties and unnecessary expense later (e.g. court, re-tendering, public relations, etc.). It often does not matter if there is failure in fact.

To ensure the organization meets the due process expectations, having a clearly defined probity process, and potentially an independent audit of probity, may be appropriate. An example outline is provided in Figure 5.4.

Probity can come with a cost, however, particularly when it overrides commercial logic, as the following public sector case study demonstrates.

1 Probity Principles

    1.1. Objectives
    1.2. Ground rules

2 Code of conduct

3 Conflicts of interest

    3.1. Declarations
    3.2. Procedures for disclosing and managing

4 Confidentiality

    4.1. Agreements
    4.2. Procedures

5 Security

    5.1. Bids
    5.2. Organizational information and documentation
    5.3. Data room
    5.4. Site visits

6 Recordkeeping

    6.1. Records of attendance and minutes of briefings, interviews, site visits, debriefings, etc
    6.2. Process of receipt, recording and acknowledging bids
    6.3. Question and response log

7 Evaluation Process

    7.1. Tendering strategy
    7.2. Establishment of criteria, extent of disclosure and management of potential alterations
    7.3. Due diligence
    7.4. Notifications
    7.5. Process of question and response information distribution

8 Approvals

    8.1. Evaluation criteria
    8.2. Selection recommendation

9 Debriefing

    9.1. Information disclosed
    9.2. Personnel authorized

Figure 5.4
Probity plan outline

Case Study: a government department

The department that managed all the office accommodation needs for the government was running a multi-staged tender beginning with an ROI, progressing to an EOI and was now in the RFT stage. In each case, the response instructions required the bidders to have their response deposited in a locked tender box by 2 pm on the specified date. The probity advisor would then unlock the tender box and deliver the responses to the secure evaluation room. Much effort had gone into culling the inferior suppliers from the initial 25 ROI responses to the final three invited to the RFT. The top shortlisted supplier's bid was four minutes late and they were not allowed to put it in the tender box. The organization was too fearful of the probity advisor to suggest the approach may have been too drastic and to this day is convinced it was forced to pick the best of two inferior bids rather than the best value for money.

5.6 Preparing the market package

The market package is the set of information submitted to the market where potential bidders will submit their offers. The offers an organization receives will reflect the quality and clarity of information provided in the market package documents. Garbage in–garbage out. If the market package, in particular the key governing documents (contract, SLA and price model), are prepared as close to the final versions as possible, the organization will increase the probability of obtaining exactly the services it requires, under the conditions it requires, and will gain considerable negotiation efficiency since little is left to chance or opportunism.

However, traditional market packages use a scattergun approach – oscillating between descriptions (i.e. background information) and requirements (i.e. questions to be answered by the bidder). This is difficult for suppliers to prepare their bid against and, later, for evaluators to map the response.

A more effective alternative is to structure the documents in 'parts' with one section containing all the information the bidder needs to know, and the other section detailing what the organization needs to know to make its decision:

- Part 1: information for the tenderer. This contains background information, conditions of tendering (including submission instructions) and information on services as they are currently performed. The SLA and contract are attachments along with any other documentation that forms the basis of the information on which the supplier is to price their offer.

- Part 2: response framework. This is the response framework and constitutes the bidder's official quotation submission. It is structured such that each question asked of the respondent maps directly into the criteria developed in the selection strategy. In this manner, the suppliers can prepare a bid that is efficient and effective to score and the evaluation team will have all the information required to give a score.

Figure 5.5 outlines the Part 1 and Part 2 style market package.

Once the market package has been prepared, there are a number of methods for distributing it:

- On-line – the internet is an increasingly popular distribution medium, whereby potential bidders are directed to a website and, after registering, can download the market package. On-line distribution offers significant productivity benefits since resources are not required to be tied-up processing requests and printing. Alternatively, market packages are also e-mailed to the registered bidders.

- Picked up by hand – bidders can physically come to the organization, sign a confidentiality agreement and receive the market package in print form or on CD. Alternatively, the market package can be distributed at a briefing after the attendees have signed confidentiality agreements.

- Post – the traditional method of mailing out the market package is always an option.

Just issuing paper documentation and expecting a skilful and comprehensive response is naive. Bidders require interaction to be effective. The more an organization assists suppliers in understanding the organization, its strategies and views, its preferred way of operating and so on, the better the responses will be. There are a number of options to consider in assisting suppliers with their knowledge gathering. Table 5.5 details six common facilitation techniques used in practice.

PART 1: TENDER DOCUMENT

1 Structure of this Market Package

2 Background
  2.1 Objectives of this Selection Process
  2.2 Overview of Services Sought
  2.3 Overview of Organization
  2.4 Service Environment

3 Instructions to Respondent
  3.1 Timetable
  3.2 Conditions of Response
  3.3 Evaluation Process
  3.4 Briefing
  3.5 Notification and Query Procedures
  3.6 Contract Officer
  3.7 Confidentiality
  3.8 Document Ownership
  3.9 Probity
  3.10 Client's Rights Regarding this
       Tender Process

4 Services as Currently Performed
  (as appropriate)
  4.1 Services Profile
  4.2 Management Profile
  4.3 Staffing Profile
  4.4 Balance Sheet
  4.5 Current Contracts/ Relationships
  4.6 Stakeholder Profile

5 Future Requirements
  5.1 Known future requirements
  5.2 Potential future requirements

ATTACHMENTS
Contract
Service Level Agreement
Operational and technical data

PART 2: RESPONSE FRAMEWORK

1 Acknowledgment

2 General Information About Company

3 Criterion 1 (from evaluation criteria)
  3.1 Subcriterion 1 Questions and
       Information Requirements
  3.2 Subcriterion 2 Questions and
       Information Requirements
  3.3 Subcriterion 3 Questions and
       Information Requirements

4 Criterion 2 (from evaluation criteria)
  4.1 Subcriterion 1 Questions and
       Information Requirements
  4.2 Subcriterion 2 Questions and
       Information Requirements
  4.3 Subcriterion 3 Questions and
       Information Requirements

          .
          .
          .
          .

5 Criterion NN (from evaluation criteria)
  5.1 Subcriterion 1 Questions and
       Information Requirements
  5.2 Subcriterion 2 Questions and
       Information Requirements
  5.3 Subcriterion 3 Questions and
       Information Requirements

6 Contract and SLA Compliance
  6.1 Proposed variations to contract
  6.2 Proposed variations to SLA

7 Price Model
  7.1 Fixed prices
  7.2 Variable prices
  7.3 Schedule of Rates

Figure 5.5 Market package outline

Table 5.5 Bid facilitation options

Type	Description
Briefings	Suppliers welcome most opportunities to meet and obtain information from the organization. At a market briefing, suppliers are usually presented with at least the following by the organization: ● Background information on the organization, its history and its future strategies ● Reasons for outsourcing, discussion of key requirements and the organization's expectations of the service provider ● Introductions to key stakeholders and their views ● An overview of the market package; evaluation criteria, key dates and further stages in the selection process ● Objectives, issues and other items which are difficult to communicate or emphasize in a voluminous market package
Questions and answers	Suppliers will always have questions throughout the response period. The typical manner to handle this is to have a written request/response procedure. Only that information required clarifying the market package sent out or other communications should be shared to other suppliers, not the proprietary information of potential bidders
Site visits	When documentation cannot adequately convey the information to prospective suppliers, bidders can be offered the opportunity to visit sites. It is appropriate that two representatives of the organization be at the site visits, as they will make representations during the visit that will be relied on by the suppliers
Workshops	Workshops can take any number of formats (brainstorming sessions, idea generation, problem solving or just gaining an understanding of how the organization operates) to enable the supplier to explore different options with the organization to better tailor the solution. Opportunities to problem solve and exchange views between the parties, particularly where there may be a great deal of interdependence, are rarely a poor investment of time and resources
Data rooms	There are some occasions where it is not practical to include necessary information and data in the market package. These occasions call for the use of a data room. A data room is a secure room containing data, bulk information and, if appropriate, a secure terminal to assist prospective suppliers with formulating their bid. The room is made available to all registered prospective bidders, each of whom are allowed an opportunity to visit the room and view the data. Bidders arrange a time for the viewing and are usually not permitted to make reproductions of documents contained in the data room without authorization

Continued

Table 5.5 continued

Type	Description
Discovery/due diligence	The objective of this process is to permit the bidders to verify the representations made by the organization in its market package and subsequent communications. The due diligence conducted by the service provider will involve clarification of the assumptions on which their proposals are based. The benefit of facilitating the supplier's discovery process is that it will limit the qualifications, disclaimers and risk contingencies put over uncertainties in their bid. The supplier's due diligence can include, but by no means is limited to, the following: ● reviewing existing service agreements, contracts, subcontracts, service provider agreements, lease agreements, supply and equipment sources, maintenance practices and related items for which the service provider will take responsibility ● verifying the inventory of all assets to be purchased, or provided by the organization, verifying the ownership, determining the condition and market value ● validating service definitions, KPIs, baseline costs, capacities, loads, backlogs ● confirming configuration, systems software, documentation, security, change control ● reviewing applicable organizational standards, policies and procedures that they will need to comply with ● confirming the employment conditions of staff that may be transferred under 'no less conditions' ● interviewing management, users and other key stakeholders ● running integration tests and diagnostics

5.7 Successful selection – ITO is not an auction

Successful ITO is not about getting the lowest price at any cost – it is about getting the lowest price with a superior supplier under a fair contract with sustainable solutions. It is not a one-off economic transaction, but an ongoing relationship with economic and strategic consequences. If the organization selects wisely, these consequences can be good; if not, they will be bad. Remember that the lowest bid is not always where the real value is, as the following experience demonstrates.

Case Study: a major retailer

The IT department of a retailing company had recently been transferred to under the Corporate Services division that had a general manager with a background in procurement. It was her belief that commodity functions should be outsourced so that the division could focus on adding value to the operational business units. She targeted the 'commodity' IT services and went to tender for the IT data-centre operations, charging $500 to suppliers to receive the RFT to weed out anyone that was not serious. The emphasis was placed on price as she believed the services, approaches and suppliers were undifferentiated. Accordingly, the lowest-priced bid was awarded the contract. This bid was 30% below the nearest bid.

Things began to go awry very quickly. Variations were the norm, in fact a person had to be dedicated to variation management. Service levels, set up as targets and not minimum standards in the supplier's standard contract, were rarely achieved. The supplier had capped the number of resources they would provide on the contract and the general manager had to hire specialists to work in the data-centre to raise service levels back to what they had been. Within a year the total costs were higher than the highest bid, higher than the in-house baseline and the division's remaining IT people were focused on firefighting, not adding value.

5.7.1 Scoring bids

Comparing the bids is the typical starting point for the competitive evaluation. Assessing the responses to the information requested can be a tedious process, but it is one that is crucial. It requires careful analysis, identification of the many points that require clarification to decisively form conclusions, and the ability to separate motherhood statements and ambiguous claims from pragmatic solutions. Accordingly, there can be many rounds of bid assessment and clarifications before the evaluation team is in a position to decisively score the bid.

The potential values that a bid can 'earn' for qualitative criteria is generally determined via two methods:

1 Ranking method – each bid is ranked from best to worst for each criterion. For example, if there are five bids, each bid receives a unique rank of 1 to 5 per criterion.
2 Scoring method – each bid is given a score for each criterion appropriate to the assessment of the response. An example scoring system can look like the one below:

0 Did not respond, non-compliant.
1 Poor response, high risk.
2 Meets most requirements, but there are some concerns.
3 Meets requirements, will work.
4 Superior response to other bids.

Furthermore, the bid as the formal response is only one source of evaluation information. In addition to evaluating the formal bids, there are a number of additional intelligence gathering methods every organization should consider. These are presentations, interviews, workshops and site visits (see Table 5.6).

Table 5.6 Evaluation process options

Technique	Description
Presentations	A market package and the resultant bid are all paper-based communications. However, true communication between people is primarily non-verbal. Consider having the bidders present their proposal to the organization, such that each supplier can highlight its bid 'in its own words'
Interviews	Interviews with the bidders help to gauge how well they understand the needs, understand what they have written, and give the organization the opportunity to ask difficult questions. It also gives an opportunity to meet the key individuals proposed in the bid and assess their personal capabilities. The success of the ITO arrangement, at the end of the day, has a direct correlation to the strength of the relationship. Relationships are between people, not organizations, thus it is critical to determine if the parties will form the right relationships at the right level driven by the right people
Workshops	Workshops give an opportunity to assess how well the parties can work together and problem solve. Opportunities to problem solve and exchange views between the parties, particularly where there may be a great deal of interdependence, are rarely a poor investment of time and resources. A workshop can be centred on solving a real-life issue the organization is facing or a hypothetical one that the parties may encounter
Site visits	Touring the supplier's operations is invaluable in obtaining an understanding of how they conduct their business. Touring customer sites that are managed by the supplier give the organization a chance to observe their relationship management in action

5.7.2 Determining the cost

The 'money' part of the 'value for money' equation is comprised of two components: (1) the quoted price, and (2) the total cost.

In all ITO arrangements other than a completely fixed-price contract, price will not be static. Different scenarios will result in different costs to the organization. Accordingly, it is very rare that a price evaluation does not include some form of sensitivity analysis. Key assumptions may alter, and this may significantly impact on the net-benefit available to the organization. Key assumptions are more than likely to change over time as potential suppliers clarify what is required and the likely risks associated. Take the best, worst and expected demand (base case) scenarios to determine the range of the bid price.

Total cost is not only the supplier's offered price (or sensitivity price range), but also includes the total cost of the transaction and contract management. Each bid may not have the same transition, ongoing management and termination costs, as such, and these very definitely need to be factored in. Table 5.7 indicates the sorts of costs to be wary of and factor in.

5.7.3 Determining 'best value for money'

Once the bids have been scored and the price range established, the organization is in a position to determine the preferred supplier. Selecting the supplier on 'best value for money' attributes rather than price alone has become the norm, particularly as organizations have learnt that lowest price does not equal lower overall cost. In fact, the opposite is often the case – the lowest price results in the highest overall cost.

This means that the organization may not select the least expensive option, or the highest qualitatively ranked supplier. Instead, it weighs price against quality to select the best value for money (see Figure 5.6). This is best determined by setting a cost ceiling (often the in-house base case) and a quality floor (the minimum acceptable score for the qualitative criteria). The viable bids then are within those thresholds. The best-value-for-money supplier can then be determined by graphing the qualitative score against the net present value of the prices offered.

Figure 5.6 shows the process at work with four different suppliers A, B, C, D. Clearly Supplier A does not fall within the minimum quality threshold and so it can be eliminated.

Table 5.7 Total ITO costs

Cost	Description
Price	The price may actually be a range, rather than one number. While there may be a fixed price component, most ITO arrangements have variable components as well
Transition costs	Making the transition to market provision can be difficult and expensive. Transition costs represent the transaction implementation costs that would be necessary to put the ITO arrangement into operation, thus must be added into the cost comparison. Such costs include: • The transition fee charged by the supplier – the organization should specify how they want this cost to be paid (upfront or over the life of the contract) • The equipment purchased, net of tax – the actual cash received will be dependent upon the difference between book value and fair market value of the assets and the organization's tax situation • The cost of the organization's transition team – each supplier tends to have different requirements from the organization depending on its transition approach. In addition, there will be the cost of verifying all aspects of the transition have been completed • Personnel costs – redundancy and leave payouts, outplacement fees, potential union litigation are the primary costs associated with the transition of staff. The costs will vary between suppliers depending on the number of staff they will take and the conditions
Retained costs	Not all IT costs related to the in scope services can be transferred to an outsourcing supplier or eliminated when an internal service is closed. Depending upon the supplier's offer, there could be sunk costs that the organization will continue to incur. Examples include: • equipment leases that are not transferable due to the supplier's solution or restrictive lease provisions • redundant resources (net of disposal proceeds) including equipment, software, contracted services that will not be taken up by the supplier • retained staff that the supplier will not be requiring, will not be made redundant and are not part of the retained organization plan – until such time as they are redeployed
Ongoing management costs	Each supplier's approach may require a different mix of management resources, hence varying costs. There will be skills required by the organization that differ from the traditional IT skills to define business requirements, negotiate and control contractual arrangements, measure performance and resolve problems. Training of current personnel or acquiring the needed skills will be required. Miscellaneous expenses will occur covering billing validation and adjustments, reporting, and clerical costs. In addition, auditing the supplier may be desirable to ensure there are proper internal controls, billing practises, and compliance with clauses such as a technology refreshment, benchmarking or price indexing

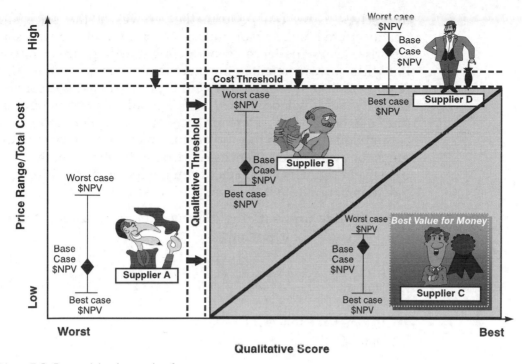

Figure 5.6 Determining best value for money

Supplier D costs too much and supplier B will be a better all-round choice. However, Supplier C scores the best by far – but it is still worth re-checking the assumptions on which this seemingly superior bid is based.

5.8 Due diligence investigations

The bid assessment and other evaluation techniques only get the organization to the stage where it believes it has the best ITO solution. At this stage it is important to remember it is still just a theory, however. Due diligence will be warranted to move out of theory into reality. Due diligence is an in-depth assessment of the preferred bidder and the bid (or the bidders included in the BAFO stage) prior to awarding a contract. It is in the organization's best interest with regard to risk management to undertake comprehensive due diligence. Rarely should the solutions or the bidding organization be taken at face value as presented in the bid.

Due diligence involves investigating the suppliers' claims that they are a sustainable entity, are what they have represented themselves to be, can perform the services at the price and quality offered in their bids and so on – to minimize unpleasant surprises. Our experience in conducting due diligence examinations has always resulted in discovery of major issues that require resolution in order to award the contract with reasonable certainty that it will be successful. We should also point out that due diligence very often protects the supplier too, from assumptions based on incomplete information, from paying too much for over-valued client assets, from inheriting a higher cost base than originally stipulated, from over-keen price bidding in a determination to get the deal at all costs.

There are five forms of due diligence the organization should consider before outsourcing:

1 Price.
2 Solution.
3 Company.
4 Customer references.
5 Contractual.

5.8.1 Price

Offering the lowest price can be intentional, but quite often it is not. Rather than a low price being the result of a careful crafted strategy, say to offer a 'loss leader' to gain other work, it can be due to oversights, omissions, incomplete information, over-simplification of the requirements, insufficient knowledge and so on. Organizations have two choices when it comes to the price offered: (1) accept it at face value and hold the supplier to it even if they will suffer the 'winner's curse' (an unrealistic and unrecoverable bid), which can result in extensive management to enforce service quality when the supplier is focused on recovering costs and increasing the margin; or (2) conduct due diligence to assess the viability of the price and the assumptions made and make an assessment as to the depth of the supplier's understanding when they made the offer.

Price due diligence investigations estimate the direct costs of service provision including, but not limited to, the following:

● Workforce proposed to staff the contract to determine that it is staffed appropriately (numbers and skills).
● Amortization of assets and refresh (if a technology refresh is part of the arrangement).
● Licences and maintenance fees.

- Travel costs if geographically dispersed scope.
- Implementation costs including reconfiguration, network installation, etc.

5.8.2 Solution

Many solutions offered may be theoretical in nature; that is, they are not currently in practice or the proposed team does not have experience in them. Perhaps aspects of the solution have not been tried and tested in an organization with a similar architecture or geographic scope. Accordingly, to ensure the solution will work, appropriate due diligence may be prudent, such as conducting systems integration tests, systems walk-throughs, site visits and the like to be assured that the proposed technical solutions will provide what was promised and will work for the organization.

Due diligence investigations into the solution assess the viability of the technical and service delivery aspects of the offer including, but not limited to, the following:

- Tools, systems and technical infrastructure.
- Operational, change management and fault procedures and processes.
- Staffing and management arrangements.
- Technical and organizational interface and integration.
- Security, disaster recovery and contingency planning, systems and infrastructure.
- Reporting and billing systems.

The following case study gives a taste of the sort of things that can be discovered during due diligence.

Case Study: a mining company

An international mining company had selected a supplier primarily based on their superior technical solution. Because the technology would be quite a strategic leap for the organization, it decided to perform a technical solution due diligence as a prerequisite to signing the contract. It quickly discovered that the supplier had not installed the technology in any geographic region in which the organization conducts its business and had no local experience in either implementation or management of the technology.

In fact, the experience was all in one US city and that team was fully booked for two years.

The US team agreed to meet with the organization to discuss implementation and management. Much to the organization's credit, they invited the supplier's local arm to attend as well. After a few workshops, the organization was even further convinced of the benefits of the technology, but was completely unconvinced of the local arm's ability to deliver it. The contract was changed from a packaged outsourcing contract to a straight technology/software purchase and the organization created a team within its own staff to learn, implement and manage it.

5.8.3 Company

An assessment into the supplier company itself is always warranted. A prudent organization never relies on a strong brand as the indicator of financial viability; it is more often the result of good, often expensive, marketing. The ITO investigation that takes place is similar, but not as extensive, as the investigation that takes place regarding a potential acquisition or merger, including ownership structure, senior management, quality certifications, detailed financial information, forecasts, customer and subcontractor dependency and so on.

Company due diligence investigations assess the viability of the company including, but not limited to, the following:

- Company profile – date of incorporation, history, services/products offered, corporate group structure, capital structure, shareholding, discontinued businesses.
- Directors and senior management – organization chart, personal profiles, related party transactions.
- Revenue – market share, turnover by service/customer/geographic segments, principle customers and relative % of total sales, current proposals.
- Accounting – annual report, external auditor, internal audit function, principle accounting system.
- Financial viability – current/fixed/intangible assets, short-term/long-term liabilities, contingent liabilities, cash flow, insurances, related entity transactions.
- Employees – number by service/customer/geographic segments, industrial relations, turnover, training.

5.8.4 Customer references

Reference checking is a mandatory procedure, in our opinion. It is a key way for the organization to find out how the supplier's customers feel about them and their satisfaction in areas that may be of concern to the proposed arrangement. The best references are those from customers that most closely resemble the organization, with an arrangement that most resembles the nature of the proposed ITO arrangement and had similar issues (i.e. implementation, integration, pricing, staff transition issues).

Customer reference checking can include:

- Gap assessment between the two entities (the referee customer compared to the organization) concerning the difference in the company profiles and scope of arrangement (type of services, geographies covered, complexity, scale, KPIs, etc).
- Reasons for outsourcing and other options considered, reasons for selecting the supplier vs. other suppliers.
- Implementation, including whether delivered on time/ budget, role of supplier and role of referee, issues that arose, etc.
- Service delivery performance, including technical integration and management, KPIs, business vs. non-business hours performance, management of subcontractors or other third parties, etc.
- Staffing, including quality of staff, staffing management, staff turnover, integration and satisfaction of transferred staff, etc.
- Contractual and SLA compliance, audit findings and resolution, variations including reasons, outcomes and management.
- Problem resolution, including types of problems, method, role of referee and role of supplier, etc.
- Retained organization originally planned and that which was needed.
- Overall satisfaction including the cost, supplier's strengths and weaknesses, relationship management, supplier meeting its representations, benefits to the organization, etc.
- Hindsight, including pitfalls, learnings and suggestions on how the referee would do things differently.

5.8.5 Contractual

This assessment ensures that all representations made and contractual obligations agreed are evidenced. It includes obtaining copies of insurances, guarantees, subcontractor agreements, certifications, etc. Just agreeing to items in a contract does not mean such items actually exist or have actually been put in place and taking a supplier to court for breach is rarely a viable option.

Contractual investigations verify that what has been agreed to in the contract exist:

- Insurances.
- Guarantees – financial and performance.
- Subcontractor agreements.
- Warranties.
- Certifications (e.g. quality) and conformance with standards.

5.9 Negotiation

So much emphasis has been on negotiation in ITO contracts that an inexperienced person could believe that it is the pinnacle of the ITO lifecycle. If it does becomes the pinnacle, then something has gone wrong in the earlier processes – usually because the organization's intent has not been sufficiently articulated by drafting the contract/SLA as part of the request for tender, the baselines on which the business case is predicated are invalid, or the supplier has radically changed their offer once at the negotiation table and the organization had not developed a feasible BATNA (best alternative to a negotiated agreement) and has placed itself in a position whereby the supplier is able to act opportunistically.

In following our building block approach, negotiation becomes a task of refining the exact wording of the governing documents, not a give and take of the intent of the arrangement. It thus becomes more a process of calculating, rather than of straightforward negotiating. The contract and SLA have already been developed and the supplier's exact preferred alternatives declared, the discovery/due diligence process for both parties has been conducted and concluded, preparation for the transition has occurred (novated licences, asset inventories, etc), the retained organization is in place and mobilized and so on.

Nonetheless, some negotiations will need to take place and the organization will have to be prepared for them. To help you here, Figure 5.7 provides a negotiation strategy outline while Table 5.8 provides vital check questions on logistics and tactics for planning negotiations. The show-stopper questions for your deal are particularly important to flush out, and we indicate some sample ones in the table.

1 Context
    1.1 Background
    1.2 Recital of Key Events

2 Overall Plan
    2.1 Scope of Negotiation
        2.1.1 Objective of Negotiation Strategy
        2.1.2 Summary of Items to be Negotiated
        2.1.3 Timetable
    2.2 Negotiation team
        2.2.1 Lead negotiator
        2.2.2 Trump negotiator (last resort)
        2.2.3 Core negotiation team
        2.2.4 Consultation personnel
        2.2.5 Approvals
    2.3 Processes to be followed
        2.3.1 Logistics
        2.3.2 Minutes of negotiation sessions
        2.3.3 Redrafting and acceptance
        2.3.4 Final authorizations and signing

3 Items to be Negotiated
    3.1 Item #1
        3.1.1 Positions of both parties and underlying drivers of the positions
        3.1.2 Win/win scenario
        3.1.3 Negotiation style required
        3.1.4 Personnel required by both parties (at the negotiation, consultation, approval)
        3.1.5 Organization's BATNA (best alternative to a negotiated agreement)
    3.2 Item #2
        3.2.1 Positions of both parties
        3.2.2 Underlying drivers of the positions
        3.2.3 Win/win scenario
        3.2.4 Negotiation style required and tactics to employ
        3.2.5 Organization's BATNA (best alternative to a negotiated agreement)
        3.2.6 Personnel required (at the negotiation, consultation, approval)

               .
               .
               .

               .

    3.3 Item #NN
        3.3.1 Positions of both parties
        3.3.2 Underlying drivers of the positions
        3.3.3 Win/win scenario
        3.3.4 Negotiation style required
        3.3.5 Organization's BATNA (best alternative to a negotiated agreement)
        3.3.6 Personnel required (at the negotiation, consultation, approval)

Figure 5.7 Negotiation strategy outline

Table 5.8 Negotiation planning questions

Logistics	Tactics	Showstoppers
• Who will be negotiating? • What role will each person have in the negotiation process? • Do any other people need to be consulted as part of the process? • How will the process begin? • Where will negotiations be held? • How long will each session be allowed to run? • What form of minutes will be produced following each session? • Who will take notes?	• What style of negotiation will be used by the other party? • What impression do we want to create? What style should we use? • Are we prepared to bluff? • Are we able and/or ready to make any concessions? • Are we prepared to use pressure tactics? How should we react to pressure tactics being applied? • How will counter offers or packages of compromise be addressed? • Does the supplier have any position of strength? Does the supplier have any weaknesses that can be exploited?	• What are the main stumbling blocks likely to result in conflict? • What are the main points of divergence? • Are these likely to stop the show? • At what point should our trump negotiator intervene? • What alternatives are there in the event that no agreement is reached (BATNA – best alternative to negotiated agreement)?

The best plans, however, cannot substitute for the communication, listening and relationship-building skills of the negotiation team. Accordingly, it is imperative that both parties are working together as problem solvers looking for solutions that leave both parties satisfied, and not conducting psychological warfare and applying pressure tactics. Some of the sorts of things that can happen during the negotiation period are hinted at in the cases described below. As a general principle for both client and supplier sides, it is important not to have one group doing the negotiations, and still another responsible for delivering the service. It is also important to have people involved who understand the practical ramifications of what is being agreed, and that can represent the interests of the stakeholders likely to be affected.

Case Study: a tale of two negotiations

After months of discussions, an international accounting firm and international equipment services company had agreed to a deal in principle. All that had to be done now was to negotiate the details. The contract and SLA was moving along fine, however the price was hitting some major stumbling blocks. The supplier's price negotiation team was led by the salesman; the accounting firm's by the finance director. The salesman wanted the deal done as quickly as possible and the finance director was not going to sign anything until the numbers were right. The salesman tried every tactic he knew of to try to get the contract signed except deliver the prices in the breakout manner requested. The finance director was growing increasingly frustrated to the point that he refused further meetings until the price breakout would be presented. When that meeting was convened, it was preceded by an hour-long presentation of the history of the relationship. The entire negotiation team of the firm by this time was visibly agitated. The firm required the removal of the salesman from the negotiation table in order to proceed. The deal was signed shortly thereafter, with the desired numbers in place.

Meanwhile, with another client, the same supplier handed over negotiations to the operations team that would be responsible for making the deal work. The operations team discarded so many of the sales team's representations, telling the client 'how things will really be', that the client was left with a deal bearing little resemblance to the one they had expected. Rather than terminate discussions, which was the first instinct of the client, the client went back to the sales team with their issues. A more commercially astute and relationship-orientated operations manager was substituted, a detailed briefing of all representations occurred, and the sales manager was included in the negotiations. The deal signed met, and in some instances, exceeded the expectations of the client.

5.10 Finalizing the contract

The last activity of this building block is to sign the agreement. Although the draft contracts (including the SLA and other schedules) were prepared in Building Block 4 ('Ensure the results: design the future') and have been refined through a competitive process (if adopted) and through negotiations, many representations may have been made during this process that have not yet been captured. The organization may be relying upon such representations — typically verbal pledges made by the supplier during the engagement process, yet these have not formed part of the agreed terms and conditions. Often these can be promises to share global 'best practice', implement some form of knowledge sharing, communicate on the latest IT trends, and a plethora of other undertakings made under the 'as part of our services to you we will . . .' banner. Failure to deliver promises appears regularly in surveys as one of the top three critical failure factors in ITO agreements (Cullen *et al.*, 2001; Lacity and Willcocks, 2000).

Accordingly, it is prudent, prior to negotiations, to finalize the contract/SLA to include the terms and conditions of these representations and work through how they will operate in practice. Therefore:

- 'Farm' or go through the tender response, negotiation, etc for 'promises' relied upon and capture them in the contract, SLA or schedules as appropriate.
- Consider implementing a balanced scorecard (refer to Building Block 4) to capture more comprehensive success criteria if representations were of a relationship or strategic nature rather than more operational pledges.
- Consider the use of a 'Relationship Values Charter' (refer to Building Block 4) as a schedule to the contract whereby the parties agree to a minimum standard of relationship conduct, if the pledges were of a behavioural nature.
- Compare outsourcing models to identify the one that has been paid for vs. the benefits that may still be expected pertaining to the other models (refer to Building Block 1 – 'Discard the myths – gather acumen'). Often the type of outsourcing model finally agreed to may not be the one originally intended; however residual expectations of a more strategically beneficial model may still exist.

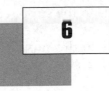

6

The sixth building block – the starting gate: make the transition

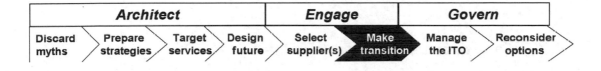

Architect				Engage		Govern	
Discard myths	Prepare strategies	Target services	Design future	Select supplier(s)	Make transition	Manage the ITO	Reconsider options

When implementing such a new way of operating that ITO represents, it is inevitable that the type of work, or how that work is accomplished, will need to change. The changes resulting from embarking on ITO are significant and will fundamentally affect the way the organization undertakes its IT functions and there needs to be careful planning and execution.

The transition process often officially begins at contract commencement and ends on a specified date or by the signing of a transition acceptance form (confirming that all aspects of the arrangement are fully operational). Irrespective of the official start and end dates, the transition actually begins much earlier and ends much later, and if not managed properly may not end at all. We have witnessed all too many deals where 'transition' becomes a permanent state. Accordingly, it is critical that the organization, in fact both client and supplier organizations, begin planning for the transition as soon as it believes outsourcing may go ahead. A good jump out of the starting gate will pave the way for a smooth process thereafter.

The key objectives of the transition are to ensure:

- that both parties are in a position to fulfil their obligations and complete specific transition actions as laid out in the contract and SLA;
- a smooth transfer of the staff to the supplier (if applicable) and their integration into the supplier's organization, systems and culture;

- a smooth transfer of the assets and obligations to the supplier (if applicable) including licences, warranties and the like;
- a smooth transfer of the third party contracts to the supplier (if applicable) including maintenance, service subcontracts and so on;
- continuity of services during transition;
- that all service levels defined in the SLA will be measured and reported as required; and
- essential business processes between the supplier's and the organization's systems are integrated.

6.1 Key transition activities

6.1.1 Previous planning

Just as the selection process is not the first building block of the ITO lifecycle (rather the fifth), transition is not the first time to plan the future strategies for the arrangement. All of the planning has already taken place, transition should merely be when the plans are executed, but allowing for the inevitable contingencies and adjustments that are needed when, as one CIO put it: 'the rubber hits the road'.

Prior to embarking on the transition building block, the following should already be in place:

- transition plan – the customer's needs were outlined in the market package and the supplier prepared a detailed response in the bid;
- disruption minimization strategy – the customer's needs were outlined in the market package and the supplier prepared a detailed response in the bid;
- communication strategy – the strategy was developed in the very early days of the ITO lifecycle;
- staffing arrangements – transfer conditions, redundancy and redeployment processes;
- retained organization and contract management function designed;
- resources mobilized – training conducted, responsibilities reallocated, etc to get the transition teams and operational teams prepared.

Check this is the case. Once again, unanticipated problems will inevitably arise if it is not.

6.1.2 Set up

The old ways of doing things will no longer be appropriate under an outsourcing arrangement. A piece of the organization has effectively been removed. New workflows, communications, paperflows and signoffs are required internally within the organization to ensure a united and efficient front interacts with the supplier. New relationships will need to be quickly formed, and people accustomed to a certain way of operating will need

Table 6.1 Example setup tasks

Setup activity	Tasks
Relationship management	• Arrange introductory meetings between key personnel • Conduct partnering workshops • Put in place communication protocols
Accommodation	• Organize temporary office accommodation for the transition team • Organize permanent office accommodation for supplier's personnel that will be located at the customer site
Access	• Arrange user profiles and security for personnel in either party that require systems access to the other party's information systems • Arrange physical access, security passes, etc for personnel in either party that require access to the other party's premises
KPIs	• Update actual baseline KPIs achieved prior to handover date • For any KPIs without historical data, design and implement measurement system • Finalize KPI reporting
Management procedures	• Finalize what processes/procedures need to be in place between the parties (arrangement procedures) • Finalize what processes/procedures need to be in place or modified within the organization (internal procedures)
Business processes	• 'As is' and 'to be' business process and technical configuration workshops • Business impact assessments • Revise flows of work, paper and communications appropriate to the changes
Retained organization	• Create new organizational chart • Redraft job descriptions • Reassign accountabilities and detail the new way of operating so that an assessment can be made of the impact on each individual • Recruit new personnel (if required) • Conduct training
Contract management	• Finalize contract management strategy and detailed plans • Conduct training for new skill sets required • Create appropriate forms • Create appropriate record-keeping and control systems

to operate in a completely different manner. Accordingly, there are a number of tasks that need to be performed to set up the ongoing operations. Eight major ones are shown in Table 6.1.

6.1.3 Transfers

The first stage of transition is typically focused around transferring assets, people, contracts, information and projects that the supplier will have responsibility for in the future. In many cases, these transfers have required dedicated teams made up of individuals from both parties because these areas of the former business were not designed to be easily transported from one organization to another. The main transfer tasks are shown in Table 6.2.

Table 6.2 Example transfer tasks

Transfer activity	Tasks
Assets transfer	• Audit inventory • Perform gap analysis from audited inventory to that listed in market package • For assets not provided for in the market package, agree ownership and separation issues • Reconcile any asset pre-payments and accrued liabilities as at handover date • Obtain copies of all asset-related documentation
Staff transfers	• Determine HR processes and policies to be used • Consult with staff on process, broad changes and approach • Consult industrial/employee relations representatives (if applicable) • Finalize staff employment with supplier • Enter transferred staff into supplier systems • Calculate settlement for entitlements and arrangement payment • Provide for supplier's induction procedures and training
Third party contract transfers	• Obtain copies of all third party contracts • Set date of novation/assignment • Prepare formal letter to third parties regarding novation/assignment date • Obtain all outstanding novation/assignment acceptances where required • For any third party contracts unable to be novated/assigned, prepare contingency arrangements (let them run out, terminate, etc)
Knowledge/ information transfer	• Conduct data and systems backup • Transfer all electronic information in the media and format required by the supplier • Conduct information exchange workshops • Walk through process flowcharts and knowledge repositories • Hand over all documentation, files and information required to the supplier
Work in progress	• Transfer current projects to supplier along with all documentation • Place order for approved projects that have not yet begun

6.2 Staff transitions

It is a common misconception that in ITO arrangements the majority of the organization's IT staff are transferred to the supplier. While this may be true for the 'mega-deals' that receive a great deal of media exposure and can involve the transfer of hundreds, if not thousands of employees, it has not proven to be the case on average. For example, in Australia, the majority of personnel remained with the organization (1997: 81%, 2000: 59%) as shown in Figure 6.1.

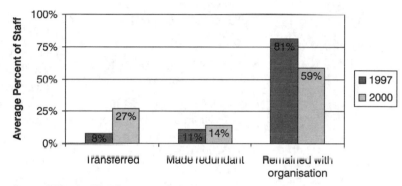

Figure 6.1
Staff employment impact

Source: Cullen, et al (2001) 75 respondents

6.2.1 Transfer options

For organizations seeking to transfer staff to the supplier, there are two general approaches to doing so:

1 Clean break – whereby the staff are deemed excess, are provided with their redundancy entitlements and their future employment with the supplier is left for the supplier to manage. In many instances the organization will facilitate supplier interviews and the like, but it will not directly participate in the process.
2 Negotiated transfer – whereby the staff to be transferred are agreed between the parties as are the terms and conditions of employment.

The advantages and disadvantages to consider when looking at these options are shown in Table 6.3.

Some of the vagaries that can be experienced with staff transfers are suggested by the case study of a telecommunications company, detailed below.

Table 6.3 Pros/cons of staff transfer approaches

Staff transfer approach	Pros	Cons
Clean break	• Less administration and communication effort because all staff employment matters are handled within one process • Speed negotiations as it represents one less complex issue to negotiate with supplier • Process equality as all staff are treated the same • Provides the supplier with the freedom to choose whom it may want to employ and under what terms and conditions • Creates a precise symbolic action for staff that have not physically moved locations to mentally cease employment with the organization.	• Highest total cost solution • Perception of allowing double dipping (providing redundancy when the individual effectively has the same job, albeit with a different employer) • Potential union difficulties as employment is not guaranteed • Negative media and potential public or customer backlash if large staff numbers are involved, particularly in high unemployment geographies • Supplier may not get all the staff required to have a viable operation and the extent of recruitment may delay the transition • 'Transmission of business' rules may be applied retroactively if brought to the courts
Negotiated transfer	• Eliminates potential severance payouts with appropriate structuring of liabilities and entitlements • Shows commitment regarding employee welfare to rest of organization • May have greater union support, if staff retain union membership and transfers are under similar or better terms and conditions • Allows organization to ensure staff are fairly remunerated	• Increases potential negotiations which can be complex and emotional • Supplier may be forced to accept more staff than it requires and cannot implement efficiencies • Can impact final price if supplier does not support the desired employment conditions and had priced its offer on different assumptions • Staff always retain the right to not accept the transfer

Case Study: a telecommunications company

A global telco had decided to use the clean break approach when outsourcing its desktop fleet maintenance function. It had employed both approaches in the past and the experiences led management to believe that it was in the supplier's best interest to let them have full control over the hiring decision and in employees' best interests to provide them a severance package. Furthermore, from the industrial relations (IR) perspective, the clean break approach released the company from any responsibility for the employees once they were hired by the supplier, whereas the negotiated transfer approach left open a possible interpretation that the company was in some manner a party to the new employment contract. The supplier had stated in their bid that they would require approximately 70% of the current workforce to transfer and had detailed a solid recruitment process, thus the transition team was fully confident that the supplier would obtain the necessary staff.

In accordance with the company policy, the IR department was handed the responsibility for conducting the clean break, and the transition team had no further involvement or, for that matter, any communication with the IR department as employee relations were considered a delicate process which was not to be interfered with by line management.

Unbeknownst to the transition team, however, it was the company's policy under the clean break approach to preclude any employee that took a severance package from working for the company for two years. This policy included working at the company under a supplier as well. Of the 300 people let go, only five took the offer from the supplier. These five were new employees for which the severance package resulted in little financial gain. The rest preferred to obtain the package and seek alternative employment.

The supplier had depended upon getting at least 70% of the staff to transfer. When this did not occur, a major recruiting drive was required. This had the effect of delaying the handover by three months until a skeleton crew was assembled. During these three months, the company had no staff in which to conduct maintenance, and thus the function was effectively abandoned. Furthermore, since the organizational knowledge also walked out the door, normal operations were not in effect for another six months. In recognition of the difficult situation the supplier was forced into, the company did not enforce the minimum KPI standards during the first year of operations.

6.2.2 Understanding the emotional impact on staff

Irrespective of the transition option the organization adopts, all IT personnel will be affected by the ITO arrangement – those that stay, those that transfer and those that require alternative employment.

Many organizations fail to realize that outsourcing can be a tumultuous change and will always have an emotional impact on employees. The 'people side' may be difficult to hear or see at first, but it will not be long before it can progress into the loudest problem that the outsourcing project may face – if it is not managed well. On some occasions, employees (sometimes in conjunction with their union) not only refuse to work but deliberately sabotage the outsourcing process. Not surprisingly, then, some of the larger suppliers have invested quite a lot of time and effort in getting their transition policies and practices well honed.

In organizational change management terms, staff that will be affected are known as 'change targets'. Organizations need to know the different behaviours that can be demonstrated by change targets so it can effectively manage the negative behaviours (such as anger and depression) that can be quite destructive if prolonged.

The following case study gives an idea of the consequences of not planning carefully enough.

Case Study: a manufacturer

John had been put in charge of outsourcing the helpdesk function of the IT department of a car maker. John's boss had clearly stated that the reason behind outsourcing was mainly to control the increasing cost of keeping up with the latest knowledge and technology. John believed that the staff in the IT department would welcome the opportunity to move to a high-tech supplier of computer services and be moved across on higher packages.

John scoped out all the technological specifications and wrote a 'Request for Tender' document. John was running ahead of the organization's timetable for these.

The Monday after the 'Request for Tender' advertisement in the paper, John was stunned when one of the helpdesk operators stormed into his office: 'How dare you sit in your office and plot all of this outsourcing to get rid of us! I bet you didn't once think about the blow you have hit us? Well I can tell you something, we are certainly not going to sit down and take this quietly, you can be sure of that.'

The scope and difficulty of this project had just changed a magnitude as John realised his mistake in not planning how to manage the people side of this ITO process. This was going to cost in time and personal stress.

To assist in recognizing what the organization is likely to come across in its change targets, below are examples of behaviours that are most often displayed, and how to deal with them.

Firstly, there is Margaret. *Margaret has worked for the organization for over 25 years, and is vehemently opposed to outsourcing. Margaret will argue very publicly against outsourcing.*

A person like Margaret may never see the benefit of outsourcing. It is an inefficient use of the organization's time to reason or use logic to sell the proposal to a 'Margaret'. In the long term, 'Margarets' will probably end up taking redeployment, early retirement, or redundancy packages rather than abide with the change.

The challenge is to not let 'Margaret' attitudes seep into other change targets and influence them against what the organization is trying to achieve. One way is to take the targets aside as a group, explain the strategy, and answer any questions they have. Give them the information needed to make an educated decision about the merit of outsourcing for them personally.

Secondly, there is Albert. *Albert was a bit stunned about the announcement, and is in two minds as to whether this will personally be good or bad for him.*

'Alberts' need to be as carefully managed as the 'Margarets' who can sway such fence-sitters. Albert's biggest concern is what he will have to do differently day-in and day-out. The organization may need to explain in detail exactly how this change will affect an 'Albert', preferably on a one-to-one basis, and effectively sell the personal benefits.

Lastly, there is Peter. *Peter has previously wondered if he would have better career prospects with a supplier, as IT is their core business. He is certain he would gain better training and a wider breadth of experience. He is anxious to get ready.*

'Peters' see outsourcing as an opportunity, not a threat. The difficulty with 'Peters' is keeping them focused on current service delivery, when they are keen to prepare their credentials and investigate opportunities with the potential supplier. However, they can assist the ITO initiative substantially as positive opinion leaders with the fence-sitters.

The model in Figure 6.2 explains the behaviours people are likely to pass through before they accept the reality of any major change. Most people will pass through each of these emotions, not necessarily in this order, and they may pass through some emotions more than once.

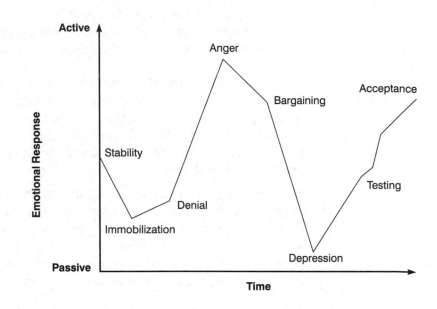

Figure 6.2
Emotional response to change model

It is much easier to manage people with the active emotions (such as anger and bargaining), as they are more visible. When people are immobilized or depressed it is harder to help them move towards acceptance. Each of these states is not only natural but also able to be anticipated by managers, and therefore plans can be drawn up about how to handle each state as it occurs. Recognize, anticipate and manage these behaviours.

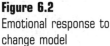

Table 6.4 Example job level impact statement (partial)

Current IT section	Current position	Type of change	New position	Deployment approach	New/key skills required
Desk top	Inventory Clerk	Elimination	–	Job pool	• N/A
	Technician	Potential transfer to supplier	Same	Clean break	• Time logging • Customer satisfaction assessment
	Procurement Officer	Job redesign	Standards Officer	N/A	• Audit • Technical writing
Helpdesk	Operator	Transfer to supplier	Customer Care Rep	Negotiated transfer	• N/A
	Team Leader	Transfer to supplier	Customer Care Manager	Negotiated transfer	• N/A
	Manager	Re-deployment	–	Job pool	• To be determined
CIO Group	–	New	Contract Manager	Recruitment	• Relationship management • Performance metrics • Commercial, legal and financial skills

The main issue that staff want to have addressed is how the ITO arrangement will personally affect them. They are less interested in what the benefits will be to the organization. Table 6.4 sets out a template for identifying what changes will occur for each individual in the organization at a job level.

To help staff come to terms with the impact, be it career impact, financial impact or even self-esteem impact, there are common techniques and services that organizations have offered. These include career counselling, outplacement, financial planning and personal counselling (see Table 6.5).

Table 6.5 Techniques for assisting staff in the transition

Staff assistance technique	Description
Career counselling	Many employees may require assistance in assessing their skills, goals and examining their future career options. Providing career counselling will help them eliminate uncertainty regarding their capabilities in the market, particularly as public sector employees may encounter a fear of working in the private sector and long-serving staff may be insecure in seeking new opportunities elsewhere
Outplacement	Outplacement services assist staff in finding new employment: first, by preparing individuals for the job-seeking process by assisting in the preparation of resumes, conducting mock interviews and the like and, second, by finding employment opportunities
Financial planning	Financial planning specialists can be hired by the organization to assist staff in assessing and making provisions for their economic situation. Often, organizations will provide one free hour of financial counselling as a service to staff potentially affected by the outsourcing initiative
Personal counselling	Outsourcing, to staff, is often an emotional issue and quite disruptive to their state of mind. Personal counselling services can assist employees come to terms with the change in circumstances and move them through the stages of acceptance

6.3 Managing the transition project

The steps outlined in this section document a complete approach for a large-scale transition. For smaller transitions, or those less complex, each step may not be appropriate. For example, there may not be a need to put in place a team responsible for the transition, but there will be a need to ensure that someone is accountable.

Table 6.6 Example transition roles

Transition role	Description
Steering Committee or a Joint Reference Panel	• guide the project and provide strategic input to the implementation process • facilitate timely decision-making and resolve issues escalated from the transition team • monitor the quality of key deliverables • provide a forum for communicating progress and achievement of project milestones
Transition Programme Leader	• manage all the transition activities across all the divisions to ensure consistency • report to the Steering Committee
Transition Project Team Leaders	• manage the transition for a specific service, geography or customer group
HR Representative(s)	• provide HR specific advice • coordinate the HR initiatives and services to staff • assist in setting up the Retained Organization
Business Representative(s)	• provide business unit specific advice • coordinate business unit transition activities • liase with business unit line management • test and accept business unit data migration and proper operational functioning
Technical Representative(s)	• provide technical advice • coordinate technical transition activities • liase with supplier's technicians • test and accept technical migration, configuration and proper operational functioning
Communications Representative(s)	• provide communication and change leadership advice • develop communications messages and media • liaise with supplier's communications representative • manage the feedback loop
Administration Resource	• coordinate logistical support • create and manage control files

6.3.1 Resourcing strategy

The types of roles an organization should consider for a transition project are shown in Table 6.6. These roles may not represent one person. Depending on the size of transition, it may be that one person has more than one role or, possibly, more than one person undertakes the same role. The formation of the transition team does not necessarily require the creation of a new team. If appropriate, it could be an existing team whose scope covers the transition. Depending on the initiative, it may be appropriate to break down the teams by division or process.

Furthermore, most of the individuals who become involved in a transition project will be engaged on a full-time basis to complete specific tasks, but their involvement may not last for the entire project duration. For others, involvement may last the entire duration of the project, but they will be engaged less than full-time.

Transition role descriptions are rarely sufficient for under-standing and preparing thoroughly for the transition, partic-ularly as there are at least two parties that need to operate in conjunction with one another. For this reason, we recommend the preparation of a responsibility matrix for transition deliver-ables that are tracked until completion (see Table 6.7). The purpose of this document is to provide a clear description of the obligations of both parties in relation to the transition.

The size and extent of the change will largely determine how long a transition will take. When scoping the timeframe, the organization will need to take into account its own unique factors – for example the amount of consultation required, the speed of decision-making, the availability and competence of line management. However, most transition projects can be accomplished if the previous building blocks were reasonably performed with 1–2 months of hard work designing the transition along with approximately 3–6 months to carry out and close out the project. You can be sure that if you are still 'in transition' after 14 months you really did not carry out a proper degree of risk assessment.

6.3.2 Risk assessment

Transitions are fraught with risks by their very nature. There can be any number of factors that pose a risk to the successful transition, examples of which include:

Table 6.7 Example transition responsibility matrix (partial)

Example deliverable	Example document reference	Managed by:		Team leader	Acceptance approval
		Supplier	Customer		
Asset condition assessment	Transition Plan xx.xx	X			
Backup	Transition Plan xx.xx		X		
Configuration documentation	Contract Clause xx.xx		X		
Data conversion tables	Conversion Plan xx.xx	X			
Interface specifications	Contract Clause xx.xx		X		
Inventory reconciliation	Transition Plan xx.xx	X			
Media statement	Communications strategy xx.xx		X		
Novation letters for 3rd party contracts	Transition Plan xx.xx		X		
Partnering workshop	Relationship Strategy xx.xx	X			
Physical access	Transition Plan xx.xx		X		
Recruitment of key personnel	Transition Plan xx.xx	X			
Service delivery procedure manuals	Contract Clause xx.xx	X			
Site tours	Relationship Strategy xx.xx		X		
Staff newsletter	Communications strategy xx.xx		X		
Staff offers	Contract Clause xx.xx	X			
Temporary accommodation	Mobilization Plan xx.xx		X		
Test data	Conversion Plan xx.xx		X		
Transition Plan	Contract Clause xx.xx	X			

- Project risks – resources skills and availability, lack of commitment from management, disparate levels of concern and priority between parties, insufficient time and resources allocated, other organizational initiatives that may have a timing impact or require resources away from the transition project, conflict in coordination between parties.
- Communication risks – mixed/conflicting messages put out by the parties, rumour drives perceptions, adverse media.
- Employee risks – employee/union action, low morale, loss of motivation, loss of key personnel, disgruntled personnel.
- Operations risks – disruptions to normal operations and service continuity, data and/or systems conversion failure, missing documentation.
- Assets risks – wrong assets moved, assets go missing, assets not in condition specified in market package, missing documentation including third party contracts and licencing agreements.
- Retained organization risks – impact of organizational change not adequately identified and addressed, required skills not available in organization or in the recruitment market.

Accordingly, it is important that the areas of hazard are identified, the consequences estimated and strategies developed to mitigate risk. Figure 6.3 gives the basics to help you design a risk assessment and strategy document. Lacity and Willcocks

Risk	Identified in processes already undertaken or yet to be undertaken
Impact	The effect the risk could have
Priority	Assigned according to their impact potential and importance to the objectives of the project
	1 – High, must be addressed immediately within project
	2 – Medium, must be addressed at specified time within project
	3 – Low, should be addressed at some point but is not imperative
Action	Recommended course of action
Responsibility	Assigned accountability to ensure risk adequately mitigated

Figure 6.3
Risk assessment strategy categories

(2001) devote a whole chapter of their book to this subject, together with case studies, should you wish to follow up on this subject in more detail.

6.3.3 Communications

It is important that the transition team communicates in an accurate and timely manner. Transition is a time of considerable anxiety for staff impacted by the change and communication is one of the most important methods of minimizing any uncertainty and anxiety. The transition team needs to identify their key stakeholders, then develop a plan to keep them informed. The objective is to provide consistent messages across the organization, so this includes keeping line management informed as well as the staff. The amount of effort that will be required should not be underestimated, as staff under stress need to hear the message several times and through different media (e.g. group, face-to-face, written).

Another key part of the communications strategy during this phase is to set the expectations of the customers or users of the service. This is particularly important if there will be changes to the service levels or a new way of operating. It is important for the organization to work with the supplier on the communications rollout such that the supplier has the full opportunity to 'sell' themselves and the arrangement to the users and understand any expectation gaps. The following case study gives an idea of how things can get out of hand.

Case Study: an insurance company

After intensive negotiations concluding with an exhaustive marathon session over the weekend prior to the handover date, the final agreement was signed. To reach the cost savings requirements of the customer, significant reductions in certain service levels were negotiated to remove the cost of maintaining a mirrored environment and having under-utilized experts on site. Each party intuitively believed that the other party would communicate the changes in operations to the users, thus neither gave it any thought. The supplier thought that the customer would distribute the SLA and manage its own organization appropriately. The customer thought that the supplier would put out some form of announcement. Each party had thought that the reaching of the agreement was the 'hard part' and were just relieved that an agreement had been reached.

After a few months of operations, the build up of user dissatisfaction was becoming alarming. Both parties were spending an inordinate amount of time dealing with complaints and had thought that the users were just 'anti-outsourcing'. After conducting a root-cause analysis of the underlying nature of complaints, it was found that the users had no emotion about the outsourcing at all, it was just never communicated to them what they should be expecting under the agreement.

6.3.4 Close-out and acceptance

It is quite common to have some form of acceptance criteria that allows an evaluation and approval process to ensure the transition has been successfully completed, it may even be in the form of a formal acceptance certificate. This is particularly important where there is a separate transition fee payable to the supplier.

Even without this formality around the completion of the transition, most organizations find it useful to conduct a post-implementation review, if only to comply with best practice project management principles. A more telling reason is that the organization will undoubtedly go through similar events in the future. Even after over a decade of publications on the 'learning organization,' learning from the present experience, and communicating that learning is an all too frequent, and costly, omission in outsourcing, as for many other organizational activities.

Part Three

Govern Phase

7

The seventh building block – get the results: manage the ITO

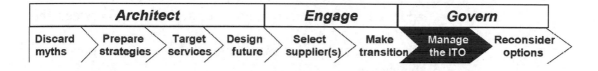

Architect				Engage		Govern	
Discard myths	Prepare strategies	Target services	Design future	Select supplier(s)	Make transition	Manage the ITO	Reconsider options

The previous six building blocks were all preparatory to this seventh stage in the outsourcing lifecycle. The work in the previous building blocks comprised the design and implementation activities necessary to make the arrangement work over the governance years. It is during this building block, that of management, that success is ultimately determined.

With the paramount importance of the technology in the post-industrial era, IT outsourcing inevitable creates a strategic partnering relationship (albeit not in the legal sense) as the organization and its suppliers acknowledge greater levels of interdependence. The successful relationship cannot be guaranteed by contracts alone. The possibility for mutual misunderstandings and unfounded expectations are boundless, as all uncertainties cannot be specified.

By virtue of outsourcing's radical shift in governance locus, new mechanisms are required for mutual understanding and trust, potential goal divergence and opportunism, redistribution of authority and decision-making, and criteria for performance appraisal.

7.1 ITO critical success (and failure) factors

Success or otherwise of ITO is contributed to by a number of factors. Outsourcing, *prima facie*, does not fail or succeed. Rather, it is the actions by both parties that will cause the arrangement to triumph or fail. Clearly, the uneconomic, inefficient and ineffective use of IT, whether the service is provided internally or otherwise, will inhibit an organization's ability to achieve its objectives.

Our recent studies have shown that there are 11 factors leading to successful ITO arrangements:

1 First – the services must be delivered not only to expectations and specifications, but improved continuously.
2 Second – both parties must have good contract management skills, processes and people.
3 Third – the relationship must be strong, with a team approach supported by a good understanding between the parties.
4 Fourth – the supplier must have quality staff and good staff management.
5 Fifth – both parties must have capable cost and financial management.
6 Sixth – the supplier must understand and listen to the customer organization and react to its needs.
7 Seventh – the vital use of SLAs and the principles SLAs are designed to achieve (clear service definitions, KPIs and performance measurement, etc).
8 Eighth – the organization must control the arrangement and processes and ensure it stays competitive.
9 Ninth – flexibility and the ability to modify any aspect of the arrangement, as required, must be incorporated.
10 Tenth – there must be ongoing and effective communication between the parties.
11 Eleventh – the supplier must provide quality technical expertise.

Table 7.1 lists these critical success factors and provides examples of how you know when things are going well on each.

The factors that lead to ITO failure, however, are not the direct inverse of the success factors. There are four major contributors to failure that regularly emerge from surveys on the subject (see also Table 7.2):

1 First – inadequate cost management, particularly when there is little flexibility within the arrangement with regard to scope.
2 Second – deficient staffing arrangements by the supplier, beginning with the supply of the wrong type of staff and continuing with poor staff management.

Table 7.1 Critical ITO success factors

Critical success factors	Examples of organizations' comments
1 Delivery performance	Improved service; timeliness and accuracy in response to work requests; maintaining systems availability; responsiveness; reliability; adherence to agreed service levels; continuous improvement; service quality
2 Good contract management	Outsourcer's management capability; improved management; commitment of senior executives; focus on management of relationship and outcomes; supplier's managers are IT professionals; overall management retained in-house; strong and active management of contract; in-house staff capable of monitoring performance; competent outsourcing/implementation project manager
3 Strong relationships	Strong personal relationships; team approach; mutual recognition of needs and capabilities; good business and commercial relationships; trust; partnership; good understanding between parties; common goals
4 Staff management	Continuity of staff; quality of individuals; availability of staff with the right skills; resolution to in-house staff turnover issues; key employees to be transferred staff; staff to be assigned to contract on a long-term basis
5 Cost management	Meeting or exceeding cost saving targets; delivering cost benefits; improved cash flow; reduced capital expenditure; value for money; profitable for supplier; clear understanding of real costs
6 Understand the customer	Supplier understands customer's business and priorities; supplier has good knowledge of customer's sites and their peculiarities; supplier gets up to speed as quickly as possible at the start of the contract; supplier understands customer's requirements; mutually understood definition of expectations
7 Use SLAs	Supplier meets service levels and reports on them; good SLA which includes clear and unambiguous service definition, service levels and responsibilities; KPIs; clarity of purpose; clear specification of benefits and ongoing monitoring of their achievement
8 Maintain control	Control of the arrangement; tender regularly – keep them competitive; clear lines of demarcation
9 Be flexible	Flexible working arrangements; ability to change; no predetermined idea (clean-slate approach); a win–win flexible contract; empathy with changing business needs; ability to vary resources to meet task requirements
10 Communicate	Clear and open communication between the parties; ongoing communication; effective communication
11 Technical expertise	Technical skills of outsourcer individuals; expertise in their field; good knowledge of job; knowledge of specific business applications

Source: Cullen *et al.* (2001)

Table 7.2 Critical ITO failure factors

Critical failure factors	Response examples
1 Cost management	Increased costs; additional costs for every 'special' instance; cost explosion; arrangement based only on cost
2 Staff	Inadequate personnel in outsourcer; wrong staff supplied; wrong skill sets; staff turnover; lack of quality staff; helpdesk staff turnover
3 Understanding	Not listening to us; not aware of who needs priority service; failure to understand business
4 Expertise	Over-estimation of supplier's abilities; over-selling and false delivery promises by sales people; lack of skills

Source: Cullen *et al.* (2001)

3 Third – the inability of the supplier to understand the organization, its needs and its priorities.
4 Fourth – the expertise gap between that expected from the supplier or promised to the organization and that actually delivered by the supplier.

Managing the four factors of failure will prevent failure, but ITO also requires pro-active management to ensure the eleven critical success factors deliver success.

Is an organization's ITO arrangement on the right track? Table 7.3 provides an extensive checklist you can use to audit the degree to which good practice has been adopted.

7.1.1 ITO management vs. IT management

There are vastly different ways in which internal provision (in-house sourcing) and market provision (outsourcing) operate. Depending on the degree of outsourcing performed in an organization, it can be a profound change in strategic and operational mechanisms, as managing outputs replaces managing inputs and negotiation replaces direct control. Outsourcing changes, or should change, the emphasis of managing service delivery from routine operations and staff management to planning, evaluating and relationship management.

The changes required in the core competencies of the IT organization and the ability to manage ITO arrangements

Table 7.3 Good practice checklist

Relationship

☐   1   Is there mutual respect and trust?

☐   2   Is there a willingness to work hard?

☐   3   Is there a continuous improvement programme and supportive mentality?

☐   4   Are both parties proactive and reactive to the other's needs and concerns?

☐   5   Is there regular ongoing monitoring and evaluation?

☐   6   Is there frequent and open communication?

☐   7   Does the IT value chain work seamlessly between all parties?

☐   8   Are there clear protocols between the parties?

☐   9   Are there demonstrable partnering attitudes and behaviours?

☐   10   Is there minimal staff turnover at either party?

Service provider

☐   1   Has the supplier delivered 'promises' made in the process of tendering, forming the arrangement and on an ongoing basis?

☐   2   Are the services and staff reliable?

☐   3   Are the skills and expertise of staff appropriate from the organization's perspective?

☐   4   Are the reports meaningful, concise and accurate?

☐   5   Does the supplier seek and address the organization's needs?

☐   6   Is customer satisfaction assessed and actioned?

☐   7   Is analysis performed to assist the organization improve its effectiveness and efficiency in the use of IT and IT services?

☐   8   Are opportunities to solve customer business issues and provide added value outside the specifics of the ITO arrangement sought?

☐   9   Is access to global knowledge and resources provided?

☐   10   Does the supplier work well with other IT service providers working within the organization?

Purchaser/customer organization

☐   1   Does the ITO management network have appropriate skills, processes and attitudes?

☐   2   Does the organization communicate its business goals to the supplier to enable it to have the strategic context for its services?

☐   3   Does the organization abdicate any of responsibilities for IT services or its obligations to the supplier?

☐   4   Does the organization recognize the service provider's right to make a reasonable profit?

☐   5   Does the organization provide early warning of major issues impacting the services?

☐   6   Is there smart and regular IT planning and involvement of the supplier in process?

Table 7.3 cxontinued

Financial

❑   1 Is value for money regularly demonstrated?

❑   2 Is price/performance competitiveness against the market regularly demonstrated?

❑   3 Are price/performance trends following general industry trends?

❑   4 Is there a level of transparency enabling the organization to assess cost drivers and react?

❑   5 Are KPIs improving over time if price is remaining static or is price reducing while KPIs are remaining static?

❑   6 Have both parties achieved their financial goals?

❑   7 Are invoices accurate and clear, with appropriate support?

❑   8 Are payments prompt?

Contractual/SLA

❑   1 Is the scope of accountabilities of both parties clearly articulated and comprehensive?

❑   2 Does the contract adequately specify both party's obligations and rights? Is it an adequate safety net for both parties in the event of something going wrong?

❑   3 Is the SLA focused on expectations and performance? Is it prescriptive only where required?

❑   4 Has a balanced scorecard approach been adopted to track and measure ITO success?

❑   5 Do the KPIs track and measure the few truly critical KPIs that drive the perception of value, not everything that can be measured?

❑   6 Are there incentives for the supplier to exceed expectations in key areas?

❑   7 Is there recourse to the organization and rectification procedures if below expectations?

❑   8 Is there flexibility to add and remove services (chop and change) based on the organization's needs?

❑   9 Is there flexibility to allow different service providers for out of scope/additional services?

❑ 10 Is there flexibility on systems, approaches and staffing?

❑ 11 Are the IT systems/processes at industry standard (current release) or industry standard – 1 (previous release)?

❑ 12 Is there matching of supply and demand to minimize paid over capacity, high cost under capacity?

---

should not be underestimated. Organizational inexperience in outsourcing is the most significant problem witnessed by organizations. From then on, as Table 7.4 culled from our own survey work shows, the majority of significant problems can be attributed to the supplier. If one thinks a little harder here, it just might be that indifferent supplier performance is a product of poor in-house ITO management. As we commented in an earlier

Table 7.4 Significant problems during contract term

Most significant problems experienced	Caused by:	
	Supplier	Customer
1 Lack of experience with outsourcing arrangements	19%	**60%**
2 Lack of understanding of your business	**59%**	10%
3 Lack of proactivity	**59%**	8%
4 Lack of responsiveness	**45%**	8%
5 Staff expertise	**42%**	26%
6 Communication	**41%**	33%
7 Inflexibility	**36%**	12%
8 Getting different suppliers to work together	**32%**	9%
9 Staff turnover	**28%**	9%
10 Failure to meet responsibilities	**27%**	14%
11 Unreliability	**14%**	0%
12 Difficulty in applying contract penalties or sanctions	10%	**15%**
13 Distrust	10%	**12%**
14 Lack of cooperation	**10%**	8%
15 Lack of fairness	**6%**	3%

Source: Cullen *et al.* (2001), 78 responses

chapter, too often we find that client organizations expect too much from the supplier, and not enough from themselves.

In no event can the organization's ultimate accountability for the services provided ever be abdicated. Outsourcing is not divestiture. The organization is responsible for how the benefits of IT are exploited, how the risks and costs associated with the IT platform are managed, and how the IT services are used from the entire supplier portfolio – both internal and external.

7.1.2 ITO management skills

As organizations increasingly move towards contracting for the provision of IT services, ITO management is becoming one of the core IT activities of overall business management. Furthermore, quasi-contracts are also increasingly being used to manage internal service provision through the use of service-level agreements or the award of in-house bids.

The use of outsourcing does not imply less effort in managing IT, only a different emphasis. In many cases, the ITO Manager handles the strategic and administrative aspects of the ITO arrangement while utilizing others as part of the ITO management network such as technical experts and lead users to perform distinct tasks. The appropriate processes and people depend on the skill set available within the organization compared to what is required and the cost/benefit of using external experts.

The skill set required to perform effective and efficient ITO management include those listed in Table 7.5.

It is also important to realize suppliers can make mistakes and the organization will need the skills to know when things are

Table 7.5 ITO management skills portfolio

Skill type	Expertise examples
Financial skills:	• **Accounting** – if open books, cost plus pricing models are part of the arrangement or if there is a user pays chargeback system • **Cost management** – assessment, modelling and tracking • **Pricing** – options and sensitivity analysis
People skills:	• **Communication** – identification of two-way needs and application of techniques • **Liaison** – interpersonal skills and networking • **Negotiation** – strategy, conduct and administration • **Organizational change** – planning and directing behaviours to achieve objectives • **Relationship management** – to transcend traditional adversarial relationships to a partnering style
Process skills:	• **Administrative** – record keeping, approval processes, distribution and control • **Forecasting** – future requirements and business change impacts • **Organizational alignment** – restructuring processes and accountabilities to meet the needs of contract execution • **Planning** – strategic and operational management and for contract end • **Problem management** – timely identification and resolution • **Project management** – setting in place and monitoring the tasks, resourcing and timing required to accomplish the activities required • **Quality management** – best practice, industry standards, etc. • **Reporting** – design and preparation
Specialist skills:	• **Auditing** – contractual compliance, internal control, performance levels and cost • **Contract law** – particularly variation, dispute resolution, remedy and termination • **Performance management** – measures, reporting, and benchmarking • **Risk management** – identification and minimization • **Technical skills** – in the services being provided to accept quotes and deliverables, assess performance, and scope requirements

not right, to query intelligently, and to evaluate information. An organization will need any number of appropriately skilled technical support people to measure performance, validate charges and improve its efficient use of the supplier's service.

Participation in the management of ITO arrangements is rarely the sole domain of one person. There is a network of individuals who are utilized as appropriate, based on the particular nature of the arrangement and the skills present in the organization. Organizations tend to have their own nomenclature for jobs within IT. Here we will posit the role of an ITO Manager. The ITO Manager (or equivalent) is the hub of the ITO management network.

7.1.3 Role of the ITO Manager

The ITO Manager role, itself, involves much more than merely administering the contract – it must ensure the arrangement achieves its strategic and tactical objectives while minimizing risks. The basic responsibility of the role is to manage the efficiency and effectiveness of the relationship, processes and performance in a systematic manner while ensuring the organization is prepared for and protected against unforeseen circumstances.

The ITO Manager should act with:

- a working knowledge of the multitude of skills required to manage the arrangement in totality, then utilize other's skills as appropriate;
- due care and diligence – never leave the organization exposed;
- authority that is clear to all relevant stakeholders; and
- a strategic and holistic perspective – outsourcing is a means to achieve goals, not an end itself.

The key to successful ITO management lies first in defining the boundaries and scope of the role, then in conducting it prudently. The ITO Manager should ensure that:

- appropriate processes are in place;
- both parties fulfil their obligations;
- desirable outcomes of the arrangement are achieved;
- maximum value is achieved throughout the contract;

- risks are appropriately identified and mitigated; and
- variations and incentives/remedies are effected as appropriate.

Accordingly, the ITO Manager should be appointed to manage all aspects of the arrangement, be involved as early as possible in the outsourcing life cycle, and be appropriately trained, empowered and briefed in regards to her/his obligations. It may well be that this role is, in a particular organization, carried out by the IT director, or someone called the contract manager. The point here is that the capability to fulfil these responsibilities should exist whatever the nomenclature used, otherwise problems set in, as illustrated by the following case study.

Case Study: a hospital

The outsourcing contract was thoughtfully prepared with ongoing contract management requirements in mind. It had clear responsibilities and performance measures, and specified a variety of regular meetings with respective attendees and agendas. The contract was assigned to an employee who had no job specifications, training, or experience in contract management with the instructions 'administer this'. She diligently rubber-stamped every invoice. Not one performance review took place and contractor reports were never opened, let alone reviewed as she did not know what to review for.

7.1.4 ITO management budget

Our experience over the last decade has indicated that ITO management is an area that can be significantly under-budgeted for, particularly when the organization cuts too deeply into its IT workforce as a result of outsourcing. Managing ITO arrangements often does not lessen the IT management effort required, merely changes the emphasis. Generally, the budget for managing an ITO contract can represent over 10% or more of the per annum value of the contract, but according to our most recent survey is more commonly 3% or less (Figure 7.1). These figures do not take into any account whether the contract is being managed effectively, however. One also finds that phenomena such as

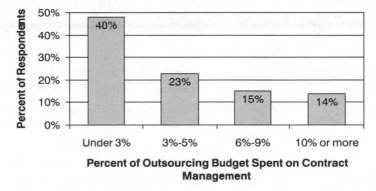

Figure 7.1
Contract management spend

Percent of Outsourcing Budget Spent on Contract Management

Source: Cullen et al (2001) 57 responses

multi-sourcing and offshore outsourcing can push up these costs significantly.

7.2 Key ITO management activities

The changing nature of contracting means that the managing responsibility transcends the traditional, more administrative role. To manage today's contracts, a direct role must be played at strategic and operational levels to ensure value for money is achieved and risks are minimized.

Depending on the nature of the contract(s), each ITO task will require a varying degree of effort and skill set, and the required timing can be on a continuous and ongoing basis or periodic in nature. Nonetheless, the full set of activities shown in Table 7.6 will be required over the life of the agreement, something that can surprise those inexperienced in ITO, as the case study below illustrates.

Case Study: an agriculture products manufacturer

After outsourcing its entire IT department of 70 people, an organization realized it did not have any personnel or processes in place to manage the arrangement. Management was not overly concerned, but called in consultants to recommend how it should be done. Over 500 tasks were required on an annual basis. This greatly surprised management who believed they had effectively washed their hands and could now reap the rewards.

Table 7.6 Key contract management activities

Activity	Description
1 Apply	performance penalties and/or rewards (if applicable)
2 Assess	need for changes to personnel, policy and procedures; changes to the SLA based on changing expectations and past performance
3 Audit	compliance with the contractual provisions, internal controls, performance, billing information, and 'open books' (if applicable)
4 Benchmark	costs and performance levels with industry standards and leading practice
5 Communicate	to stakeholders what they want to know
6 Document	all formal and informal communications within the organization and between the parties in a systematic manner that provides an audit trail
7 Evaluate	the balanced scorecard measures, performance and cost over each reporting period and over the life of the contract
8 Forecast	volume and capacity of services required and cost
9 Implement	variations to contracts and documentation to reflect changes in best practice, requirements, performance levels, etc
10 Improve	interfaces, workflows, communication and the relationship
11 Liaise	with internal management and users and between the parties regarding issues and feedback
12 Maintain	knowledge of emerging technologies, industry standards, market prices, supplier use of subcontractors, and of changes to the supplier's financial and organizational situation that may affect the contract
13 Meet	regularly with both parties regarding strategic, performance and operational issues
14 Monitor	performance levels, volume levels and the organization's effective use of the contractor
15 Negotiate	desired changes to the arrangement, the way service is being delivered
16 Plan	any potential changes to both organizations and the impact on their objectives and the services provided
17 Prepare	service and business continuity in event of service or contractor failure or disasters and for the end of the contract, both the conclusion of the natural term or early termination
18 Report	achievement of strategic and operational goals of the outsourcing process and the contract arrangement itself
19 Resolve	misunderstandings, conflicts and disputes
20 Streamline	extraneous reports, KPIs and procedures
21 Structure	management/operational accountabilities and processes internally and between the parties
22 Verify	invoices for payment and appropriateness of variation requests by either party

7.2.1 Reporting

Reports serve as analysis summary tools, evidencing the degree of success of the arrangement, providing key performance and operational indices, and identifying areas for improvement. There are a variety of reports prepared throughout the life of an ITO arrangement, typically specified in the SLA. These have been noted in Building Block 4 – 'Ensure the results: design the future'.

The reporting framework is part of the Architect Phase, as an organization is in the best position to establish the reporting mechanisms before outsourcing, not after. In many cases, reports require information that neither the organization nor the supplier currently collects data for. Even though both parties have agreed a reporting framework, the actual ability to produce meaningful data can be only theoretical until this building block. For this reason, implementing robust measurements and reporting mechanisms before an organization outsources is the ideal situation. Service level obligations are only as meaningful as the ability to report them.

The reporting cycle needs to be short enough so that significant under-performance issues can be identified on a timely basis, but long enough so that neither party is over-burdened with information preparation and review. Furthermore, a rolling cycle of reports is preferable to remain abreast of the success of the arrangement during the life of the contract.

7.2.2 Meetings

Receiving and reviewing reports is not sufficient in itself. Face-to-face contact is critical in any successful relationship, and a partnership style cannot occur without it. The parties have to be acting in concert; as running and maintaining the arrangement is an ongoing collaborative process that requires working as a team. Neither party needs to, nor should, solve problems alone.

There are a variety of meetings conducted throughout the life of an ITO arrangement, typically specified in the SLA. These have been noted in Building Block 4.

The meeting framework is part of the Architect Phase, as an organization is in the best position to establish the interpersonal communication and problem-solving mechanisms and the required participation of both parties before outsourcing, not after.

7.2.3 Evaluating performance

The evaluation of the supplier's performance is critical to ensuring the organization is obtaining what it is paying for, particularly as the planning and evaluation function of ITO management replaces the direct control over IT staff the organization had under insourcing.

Reviews focused on the supplier include, but are by no means limited to:

- cost and service performance relative to the agreement, but also relative to industry norms;
- the degree to which the supplier's obligations to the organization are met;
- compliance with the SLA and the contract;
- improvement initiatives implemented; and
- user and other stakeholder satisfaction with services.

Case Study: a homewares manufacturer

To facilitate a benchmarking exercise, a reconciliation was performed between the performance reports provided by the contractor and the reporting requirements specified in the SLA. The review found that the contractor was only reporting two-thirds of what they had agreed to. Unfortunately, this reconciliation took place near the end of the contract and the data was not obtainable.

Monitoring should not be limited to performance. With the continuous improvement and quality initiatives common to most organizations, the supplier must report on their initiatives regarding the contracted services. Furthermore, by having an 'issues to be brought to the attention of management' or similar section of the regular reporting cycle, complete with the supplier's recommendations, the organization can identify issues and improve on its part of the relationship. Figure 7.2 provides the basis for developing a supplier

SUPPLIER PERFORMANCE EVALUATION FORM

CONTRACT NO: _____ SUPPLIER: _____

ITO MANAGER: _____ EVALUATION REPORT No: _____ DATE: _____

1 SERVICE QUALITY	Comment	Score		
Understanding of requirements		0	1	2
KPIs met		0	1	2
SLA understood by staff		0	1	2
Reworks required		0	1	2
Non-conformances		0	1	2
Non-conformances corrected promptly		0	1	2
Passed Audits		0	1	2
Sub-total				

2 CUSTOMER SATISFACTION	Comment	Score		
Satisfaction survey results		0	1	2
Complaints received		0	1	2
Excessive/regular complaints		0	1	2
Complaint handling		0	1	2
Complaint reporting		0	1	2
Complaint reduction strategies		0	1	2
Sub-total				

3 COMMUNICATIONS	Comment	Score		
Reporting timeliness		0	1	2
Reports comprehensive		0	1	2
Advice		0	1	2
Problems, delays and progress reported		0	1	2
ITO Manager kept informed		0	1	2
Sub-total				

4 PROCEDURES	Comment	Score		
Procedure documentation up-to-date		0	1	2
Procedures understood by staff		0	1	2
Compliance with procedures		0	1	2
Passed Audits		0	1	2
Sub-total				

5 RISK ASSESSMENT	Comment	Score		
Disaster recovery planning		0	1	2
Service disruption minimization		0	1	2
Security		0	1	2
Internal controls		0	1	2
Site condition		0	1	2
Passed Audits		0	1	2
Sub-total				

TOTAL SCORE: _____

Scores are awarded as follows: Not achieved–(0) Partially achieved–(1) Fully achieved–(2)

Figure 7.2 Example performance evaluation form

performance evaluation form. The secret of design is to focus on significant areas in an administratively feasible way.

ITO management involves reviewing not only the supplier's performance but also the organization's own management effectiveness. The uneconomic, inefficient and ineffective use of IT, whether the service is provided internally or otherwise, will inhibit an organization's ability to achieve its objectives. The greatest efficiency and effectiveness gains are often in how the organization plans for and uses the supplier's services.

Internally focused reviews include:

- progress towards the achievement of ITO objectives;
- determination of ongoing value for money;
- degree the organization is meeting its obligations to the supplier;
- efficient use of the supplier's resources;
- effectiveness of the ITO management function and network; and
- improvement initiatives implemented.

Case Study: an insurance company

Just for assurance, a Contract Manager decided to use a redeployed systems programmer to review processing consumption and related billing. The programmer obtained recent source data and discovered that the wrong times for peak and off-peak usage were used, and batch programs that were being run at the more expensive peak times if capacity was present. How long this had been occurring was anyone's guess – old source data had long been deleted.

7.2.4 Auditing

Audits over supplier's operations can be complicated by the presence of other customers and their privacy rights, and by the increased complexity of the supplier's environment(s). Furthermore, depending upon the specific audit rights agreed to in the contract, the organization may not be able to obtain unrestricted access, may not be able to conduct surprise audits and may need to negotiate the degree of assistance the supplier must provide (and may be required to pay for such assistance).

For this reason, it is common that the supplier will hire an independent auditor to prepare an audit report for the customers. However, caution is required with these reports. Many state that 'nothing came to our attention' during the auditor's review, but do not state what controls were evaluated or the audit techniques used. Neither do they state if, or how, the controls were tested. In order to use these reports in a proper manner, the organization must understand the audit objectives, programme and procedures to determine if reliance can be placed on them.

Having each purchasing organization perform its own audits can be expensive for everyone involved, particularly since many of the audit tasks are similar across organizations. For this reason, some suppliers facilitate the formation of a 'User Group Auditing Authority' comprised of representatives from participating organizations, the supplier and all the parties' auditors (internal and external auditors). This Authority establishes audit priorities and programmes, and employs independent auditors to conduct one audit on behalf of all the participating organizations. In addition to the economies of scale this provides, it also provides economies of scope in that specialist expertise can be obtained which may not have been cost effective for each organization acting on its own.

There are three types of audits that are typical in an ITO arrangement:

1 Internal controls
2 Compliance
3 Calculations

1 Internal controls within the organization itself and those that the organization is relying upon at the supplier.

The organization can implement its own internal controls over the outsourced services, rely on the supplier's internal controls, or a combination thereof. The *US Statement of Auditing Standards (SAS) 70* is the de facto global standard regarding special purpose reports on internal controls at service organizations.

2 Compliance with contractual and SLA provisions.

Many organizations assume that if an obligation has been made in a contract the supplier will comply with it and no further work needs to be done. However, astute organizations do not assume compliance, they ensure it.

Typical clauses that require periodic compliance audits include:

- asset maintenance – frequency and nature of maintenance work;
- bank financial guarantees – existence, amounts and provisions;
- confidentiality and security procedures – over the organization's on-site and off-site data, the supplier's staff and operating environment and over communications to outside parties and individuals;
- disaster recovery planning and testing – is being conducted reflecting the requirements of the outsourcing agreement;
- employment conditions for transferred staff;
- escrow – the items to be placed in escrow have been done so and the escrow agreement signed is one that reflects the requirements of the outsourcing agreement;
- insurance – public liability, professional indemnity, occupational health and safety and others are in effect for the period, amounts and conditions reflecting the requirements of the outsourcing agreement;
- licence transfer options – that any software and hardware licences have novation and assignment clauses reflecting the requirements of the outsourcing agreement, in particular the termination provisions;
- performance guarantees – that the performance guarantee has been signed by the appropriate parties and has the terms and conditions reflecting the requirements of the outsourcing agreement, in particular the breach provisions that can invoke the performance guarantor to continue the contract;
- use and controls of subcontractors – including back-to-back agreements, nature of work performed, workforce employment agreements and processes.

Writing airtight clauses is only effective if the supplier's obligations are put into effect and maintained as agreed. The time to discover the supplier has not done so is not when the organization is seeking to invoke the clause, as the next case study illustrates.

> **Case Study: an applications contractor**
>
> An application development and support contractor went bankrupt and discontinued operations. Under its standard outsourcing agreement signed with a number of customers, it was required to maintain source code and documentation in escrow. Furthermore, it was to ensure that its software licences were transferable in the event of insolvency. It had done none of these things. Development customers had to start applications over from scratch and support customers were forced to run applications that could not be modified without unacceptable risk.

3 Calculations of charges and performance levels by the supplier.

Verifying that charges are valid is another core function of ITO management. While each invoice is typically reviewed by the ITO Manager or designated personnel prior to payment, the source data used to bill should be audited periodically or assessed prior to payment by an appropriately skilled person. The more complex and variable the price structure is, the more auditing that may need to be performed.

The supplier typically prepares performance reports. Beyond the fact that suppliers have an inherent aim to have results presented in the most favourable light, reports can be in error or produced from inappropriate sources. Periodic audits of the source data used in performance reporting will insure that the organization is obtaining the levels it purchased.

7.2.5 Benchmarking

While most organizations perform some form of benchmarking as part of the letting of a contract, prudent contract management continues this process throughout the life of the agreement. Benchmarking can be a difficult and expensive process regardless of how IT services are sourced, internally or externally. Furthermore, the benchmarking provisions within ITO contracts are some of the most difficult ones for the parties to form and agree upon. For these reasons, it is most common that an organization will find a 'benchmarking

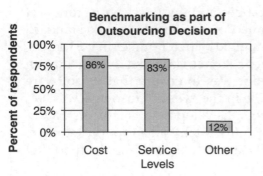

Benchmarking as part of Outsourcing Decision

Source: Cullen et al (2001) 150 respondents

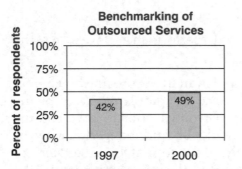

Benchmarking of Outsourced Services

Source: Cullen et al (2001) 175 respondents

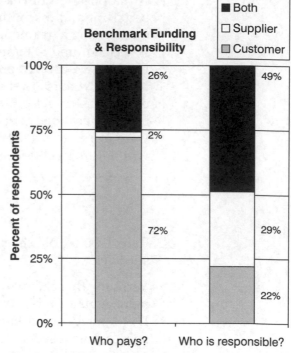

Benchmark Funding & Responsibility

Source: Cullen et al (2001) 103 and 184 respondents respectively

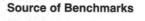

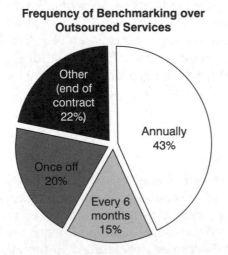

Frequency of Benchmarking over Outsourced Services

Source: Cullen et al (2001) 126 respondents

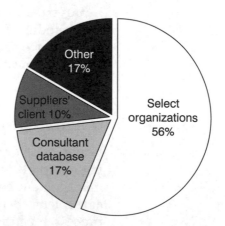

Source of Benchmarks

Source: Cullen et al (2001) 75 respondents

Figure 7.3 Benchmarking

partner' – another organization bearing enough similarities to the contracted services to allow meaningful comparisons.

Figure 7.3 provides some useful data on frequency and other aspects of benchmarking during ITO. Nearly half of organizations are benchmarking outsourced services – typically once a year, by either or both parties but paid for by the client using other select organizations as the source of the benchmarks.

7.2.6 Document administration

One of the main functions of contract administration is to have a systematic repository and log of records and decisions. Maintaining diligent administration provides an efficient reference system and audit trail should any aspect of the arrangement be called into question by either party or an external body (i.e. a regulator). Examples of the items requiring control files include:

- precursor documents (request for tenders, bids, etc);
- agendas and minutes of meetings;
- correspondence and discussions between the parties;
- approvals and signoffs;
- deliverable acceptance forms (if used);
- governing documents and variations;
- issue logs;
- reports – performance, progress, audit, etc;
- all financial data;
- supplier invoices and quotes;
- customer satisfaction surveys;
- audit reports and findings.

One of the ITO Manager's core document administration functions is to ensure that results of re-negotiations, the outcomes of resolved issues, and current practices are reflected in the governing documents. Variations are a natural occurrence – taking place continuously in procedure manuals, frequently in SLAs and occasionally in contracts. A formal process for issuing and tracking variation requests and resolutions is a core component of good governance. In Figure 7.4, we provide a sample variation request sheet. The advantages of documenting variations are illustrated in the utility case below.

Variation Request

Variation Request ID:	Raised by:	Date Submitted:

Variation Request Title:	Priority: ☐ High ☐ Medium ☐ Low Priority Rationale:	Documents Affected: ☐ Contract ☐ SLA ☐ Price schedule ☐ Other contract schedule _____ ☐ Procedure Manual _____

Description of Proposed Variation:

Justification for the Variation:

Implication of Not Making Variation:

Related Variation Requests:	Information/background Attachments:

Investigation/further work required:

Approved for Investigation (Y/N) Investigation Assigned to: _____	Resolution Approved by: _____ Date Resolution Approved:

Description of Resolution:	Variation: ☐ Approved ☐ Rejected ☐ Deferred until _____

Comments:

Figure 7.4 Example variation request sheet

Case Study: a utility

The contract had been running for a year when the service provider changed account managers. The new account manager immediately started to change services and cut some out entirely. All her actions were in complete alignment with the originally agreed contract. However, early discussions between the parties had developed and agreed to the current practices. The contract manager had documented all discussions and was able to produce evidence. All services were re-instated and both managers then made appropriate variations to the governing documents.

7.2.7 Re-negotiation and managing variations

The ability of the ITO manager and the ITO management network to re-negotiate is a core competency requirement. Formal re-negotiations are likely to take place at least annually, but more frequent and less formal re-negotiations will occur on a regular basis. As Figure 7.5 shows, and one would expect, the SLA is re-negotiated more frequently than the contract because it is designed to be a living document.

Re-negotiation may be appropriate when the following events take place, or are expected to take place:

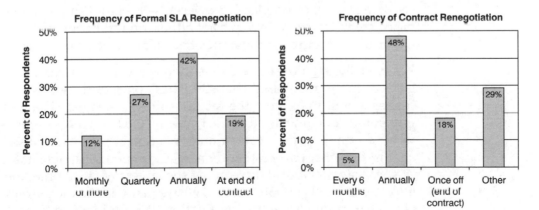

Source: Cullen et al (2001) 188 respondents

Source: Cullen et al (2001) 55 respondents

Figure 7.5 Frequency of re-negotiation

- a significant restructure of the organization – merger, acquisition, divestment, reorganization, expansion, etc.;
- expected demand levels have changed – either to a much larger or smaller extent;
- a change in the IT architectural blueprint/strategy – either a rationalization, new platform(s), new enterprise software, formation of an SOE (standard operating environment), etc.;
- a desire by the organization to backsource certain services – either because the organization wishes to rebuild the competence or believes the services are best performed internally;
- to change services levels – either appreciably upgraded or downgraded based on the supplier's performance or the organization's business requirements;
- to incorporate further services – that were not foreseen or are currently out-of-scope;
- to rectify accountability concerns – if actual operations of the arrangement have lead to resources or activities being duplicated or omitted;
- to refresh the entirety of the agreement – either because there have been extensive variations or the agreement is not meeting the needs of either or both parties;
- to rectify defects in the agreement or introduce outsourcing good practice – by including KPIs that reflect a balanced scorecard approach, introducing financial incentives, etc.; or
- to revise the pricing arrangement – to variabilize fixed prices, to fix stable variable prices, etc.

7.3 Relationship management

In most cases, the organization will want a balance between the two extremes of a completely power-based relationship and one based solely on trust. Extremes of either are rarely adequate for either party. Figure 7.6 illustrates the polar positions.

Whether the relationship exhibits more power-based characteristics or more trust-based characteristics, long-term success will be dependent upon how the relationship is managed. The best governing documents (contract, SLA, etc.) merely become weapons in a poorly functioning relationship – to be used against the other party rather than to guide successful outcomes. A successful relationship requires the investment of time and effort at all levels of both parties, where many times the journey is more important than the destination. It is an investment well worth making to establish a fundamental understanding of each party regarding the other, to establish key interpersonal relation-

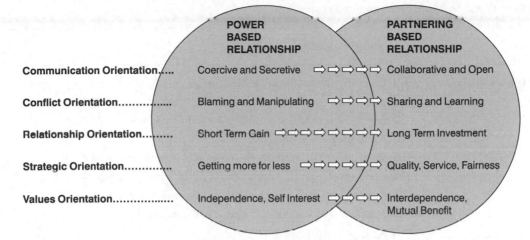

Figure 7.6 Trust vs. power relationship diagram

ships that will overcome the inevitable hurdles, and to establish the values that are shared between the parties and those that are not shared, but provide important insight into the other party.

Given the importance of the relationship, in Table 7.7 we provide a 'health check' diagnostic to assist organizations in determining whether their ITO relationships are exhibiting healthy vital signs.

Partnering is a term common today to express the type of relationship that many organizations desire. However, the concept of partnering means different, and often conflicting, things to each party. Suppliers can often use the term to mean the relationship should be based on blind (as opposed to earned) trust, to infer that price variations should be accepted irrespective of what was bid, and to expect to be the service provider for all future IT work – and they can react antagonistically when other suppliers are awarded work, and will not communicate or share cost savings achieved unless specifically directed to in the contract. Customer organizations can use the term to mean risk transfer rather than risk sharing, and can infer that partnering allows for indefinite scope-creep (inclusion of out-of-scope services) to the customer's advantage. Customers often speak of the need for partnering but do not always put in place mechanisms or processes that could encourage partnering behaviour; for example, not incorporating the supplier into the IT planning and strategy processes, retaining only a penalty-based KPI scheme rather than an incentive one.

Table 7.7 Relationship health check diagnostic

Category	Diagnostic questions
Behaviours exhibited	❑ Do both parties display ethical behaviour?
	❑ Is there an 'us' vs. 'them' mentality?
	❑ Are there unfulfilled promises by either party?
	❑ Are both parties proactive?
	❑ Does either party blame the other when problems arise?
	❑ Does either party misrepresent the relationship to others?
	❑ Do the parties give each other recognition when it is due?
	❑ Are there key individuals who dislike each other?
Perceptions of the parties regarding one another	❑ Do both parties respect one another?
	❑ Do both parties think the other party is a good listener?
	❑ Do both parties believe the relationship is a role model for the industry?
	❑ Do both parties use the relationship as an example of good practice within their respective organizations?
	❑ Are both parties reliable?
	❑ Does either party think the other party isn't pulling their weight? Living up to their accountabilities?
	❑ Do both parties think the other party is considered trustworthy?
	❑ Does either party display the NIH (not invented here) syndrome (i.e. 'it's not our problem, it's their problem')?
	❑ Do both parties understand each other's business, underlying drivers and motivations, politics?
Investment in the relationship	❑ Are both parties investing management time and effort?
	❑ Are there solid relationships at all appropriate levels?
	❑ Does each party get the management attention it needs from the other?
Communication	❑ Is there regular communication?
	❑ Is there regular feedback?
	❑ Do the parties provide early warning to each other?
	❑ Do the parties suggest improvements to one another?
Relationship processes	❑ Are there clear protocols between the parties?
	❑ Does each party assess the satisfaction of the other party?
	❑ Do the parties plan together?
	❑ If the contract has financial rewards for superior performance, have they been given?
	❑ If the contract has financial consequences for poor performance, have they had to be applied more than once?
	❑ Do the parties continuously seek better ways of doing things?
	❑ Is the organization a customer reference site for the supplier?

Both parties misuse the term to take shortcuts in the building blocks, even to the extent of believing a contract or SLA is not required, and is unnecessary with a 'trust-based' relationship. However, this results in a relationship without a sound commercial base or clearly articulated and agreed expectations. Furthermore, rarely does either party invest the time and effort required for a true strategic relationship, not least because of the day-to-day pressures of just keeping the service running. One must be on constant guard in outsourcing for ways in which the urgent drives out the important, the tactical the strategic.

Fundamentally, a partnering style of relationship infers a degree of flexibility for both parties to problem solve together. However, the exact nature of the partnering style of relationship that the parties wish to adopt should be articulated and agreed.

The contract and SLA are important, but relatively superficial drivers of day-to-day behaviour. As we try to show in Figure 7.7, true behaviour drivers are the underlying values held by the individual parties and the people involved in the agreement.

The 'Relationships Values Charter' (refer to Building Block 4 – 'Ensure the results: design the future') can articulate the desired

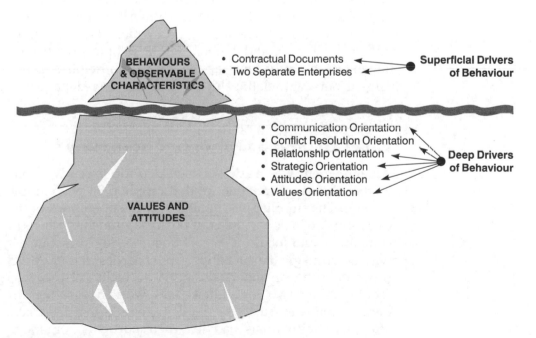

Figure 7.7 Getting below the surface

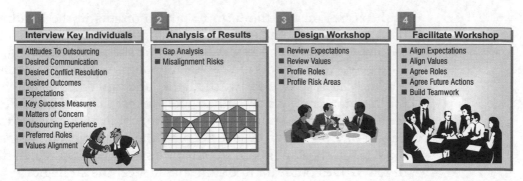

Figure 7.8 Example gap analysis process

behaviours, but in strategically important relationships organizations can benefit from ensuring the underlying values are aligned. A values gap analysis has proven useful in the past where the success of the relationship was the key to the success of the entire arrangement. The process is illustrated in Figure 7.8.

As important as the relationship is, it should not be relied upon in lieu of having proper governance in place. Relationships are between people, not organizations, and people leave organizations. If there is not a proper governance structure and procedures which exist independent of the relationship, far too much reliance can be placed on the 'unwritten understanding' which can be difficult to evidence, and which also has a habit of changing over time and with different people involved. The following case study hints at the sort of difficulties that can emerge if personal relationships in ITO are over-depended on.

Case Study: a transport company

An agreement was made between two top executives, one at the company and one at the supplier. It was simple enough. The supplier was to take over the operations of the call centre, which was its core business, and the transport company could focus on its core business, logistics. Since it was a 'strategic partnership', both parties felt a MOU (memorandum of understanding) was really all that was required. The two individuals had worked together for decades and the trust was implicit. Years down the track, after both individuals had left their particular organizations, an internal audit came up in the normal course of business. The first finding was that there was not a contract. The second, and more telling finding was that the supplier had been double-billing for years. Each business unit was being charged a price per call from a standard price schedule for the allocated volume of calls, and full cost recovery was being billed via the centralized accounts payable section. Neither organization could determine why this disparate billing process had occurred and the remediation process was extensive, to say the least.

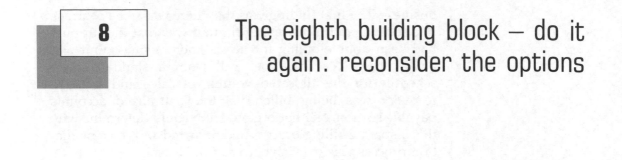

The eighth building block – do it again: reconsider the options

8

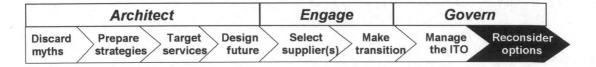

Architect				Engage		Govern	
Discard myths	Prepare strategies	Target services	Design future	Select supplier(s)	Make transition	Manage the ITO	Reconsider options

It is inevitable that the contract will end – either through early termination or by reaching the natural end of its term. The end of the contract, in whatever manner, represents the completion of the lifecycle of the current outsourcing initiative and the start of the next.

Whichever way services are provided, internally or through the market, the choice ought not to be regarded as fixed. Both firms and markets change over time in ways that may render an initial decision inappropriate in a current context. The degree of uncertainty may be diminished, market growth may support competitive (large number) supply relations, supplier capabilities change, and information disparities between the parties may diminish. Thus, any organization should periodically reassess its sourcing decisions.

An organization must give itself plenty of time to conduct this phase. Thus, the UK Inland Revenue gave itself nearly two-and-a-half years to contemplate the end of its ten-year deal with EDS. Consider the 'drop dead' date to be one year before the initial contract term expires, as any tendering activity usually requires at least six months. Even with starting at that time, an extension may still be necessary (but not for a full subsequent term). The goal is to have the next arrangement, if applicable, in place before the initial term expires and the handover date of the new arrangement either on, or before, the termination date of the previous arrangement.

8.1 Termination triggers

Generally, termination, other than the expiry of the contract, can be as the result of changes in control of the supplier, for convenience, insolvency, offence, breach, or default (Table 8.1). There may also be particular terms in the contract permitting termination in certain circumstances; for example, East Midland Electricity terminated its agreement with Perot Systems early by invoking a clause allowing this to happen in the event of a merger between East Midland and another company.

Not all ITO contracts allow the organization the right to terminate without cause (voluntary termination), although it is becoming the norm. It is useful because it is difficult to predict the future. Thus the ability to escape a contract that will not meet the future needs of the organization, even though the supplier has 'done nothing wrong', can be appealing. Nonetheless, voluntary termination often comes at a price, as can be seen in the study of 19 contracts with voluntary termination clauses shown in Figure 8.1. Over 75% of voluntary terminations would see the client paying the per annum contract value or more.

8.2 Options

There are three fundamental options with regard to the 'go forward' decision, once the new scope and new contractual framework have been finalized:

1 retain the incumbent supplier for all or part of the scope – renew the existing arrangement (rollover) or re-negotiate the new arrangement with the incumbent;
2 re-tender all or part of the scope – which may result in retaining the incumbent supplier and/or employing other suppliers for all or part of the scope depending upon how the market package is bundled and which bids are successful; or
3 backsource all or part of the scope – bring services back in-house.

In Table 8.2 we pinpoint the usual situations in which each of these might be a desirable process.

In practice, all options take place. Some services are back-sourced, some eliminated, some the incumbent supplier provides, and some a new supplier provides. To what extent this occurs varies widely. Figure 8.2 is based on Australian evidence

Table 8.1 Termination triggers other than contract expiry

Trigger	Examples
For insolvency	• a liquidator, provisional liquidator, receiver, receiver and manager, official manager, administrator or controller of the supplier or any part of it is appointed; or • an order is made for the winding up or dissolution without winding up of the supplier, or a resolution is passed for the winding up of the supplier; or • the supplier enters into any arrangement or composition with creditors generally or any group of creditors; or • the supplier is unable to pay its debts as and when they fall due or is unable to pay its debts; or • any other event or series of events, whether related or not, exists or occurs (including, without limitation, any material adverse change in the business, assets, management or financial condition of the supplier) which in the opinion of the organization would affect the ability of the supplier to comply with any of its obligations under the contract
For offence	• the supplier or any of its workforce is convicted of any criminal offence that impacts on the business of the supplier; or • the supplier is found to have falsified a claim for payment from the organization; or • the supplier is found to have committed fraud or misrepresentation
For breach	• the supplier refuses to allow the organization to conduct an inspection or audit or review; or • the supplier fails to comply with or carry out any lawful instructions of the organization; or • the supplier fails to meet any KPI minimum standard as specified in the breach provision within the service level agreement; or • the supplier fails to adhere to contractual and statutory safety standards
For default	• the result of any audit performed by the organization in accordance with the contract is, in the reasonable opinion of the organization, unsatisfactory; or • the supplier defaults in the performance or observance of any of the terms and conditions of the contract; or • the standard of work performed by the supplier is unsatisfactory; or • the time taken to complete the work is unsatisfactory; or • satisfactory safety precautions are not taken; or • by making insufficient progress with regard to quantity of work; or • by failing to communicate with customers and other members of the public in a satisfactory manner; or • by failing to perform the services or parts of it in accordance with the contract; or • by failing to properly maintain equipment used in the services
For change of control	• there is any change in the control of the supplier
For convenience	• if, in the reasonable opinion of the organization, it determines, in its absolute discretion, that there is a need to terminate or suspend the contract for the organization's business purposes

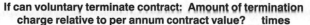

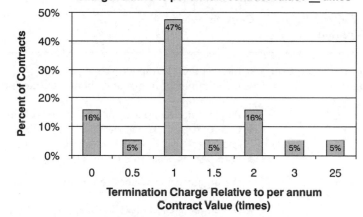

Figure 8.1

Voluntary termination charges

Source: Cullen et al (2001) 19 contracts

only, but shows that the most common end of contract process is to extend the contract in some capacity rather than re-tender, bring back in-house or terminate.

The results of the end of contract process also show that, while a prevailing number of services are retained with the incumbent, 76% of respondents gave at least some services to an alternative supplier and 41% brought at least some services back in-house. What this means is that you must ensure you have all options open, as it is likely you will want to use all of them for the renewed sourcing solution.

8.3 Assessments

To be able to evaluate the best option going forward and determine a new set of expectations, the organization will need to undergo the same series of assessments conducted in the Architect Phase, but now armed with the benefit of hindsight and experience. Most organizations that have been through at least one outsourcing cycle can approach these assessments in a different manner than a novice outsourcing organization because of the knowledge and hindsight gained from the first wave of outsourcing – thus, focusing on 'surgical strikes' throughout the building blocks.

The assessments from the Architect Phase that should be considered by any organization facing the end of a contract are as follows:

Table 8.2 End of contract options – considerations

End of contract process option	Consider when:
1 Retain the incumbent supplier	<ul><li>there is little change to scope;</li><li>the supplier provides at or below market prices and these can be demonstrated;</li><li>the supplier has performed at or better than the specified KPIs;</li><li>both parties will save significant time and effort by not re-tendering; and</li><li>both parties wish to continue the relationship</li></ul>
2 Re-tender	<ul><li>the organization wishes to ensure the most competitive price is obtained;</li><li>the scope has changed significantly and the organization believes other suppliers may have greater expertise;</li><li>the incumbent supplier will not accept the organization's revised contract/SLA at the desired price; or</li><li>the probity rules the organization must comply with or has adopted dictate a re-tender</li></ul>
3 Backsource	<ul><li>the organization wishes to rebuild its competence in the area; or</li><li>the organization believes the service is more effectively or efficiently provided internally</li></ul>

1 Contract assessment.
2 Whole-of-life arrangement assessment.
3 Knowledge refreshment assessment.
4 New requirements assessment.
5 Options assessment.

Let us look at these in more detail. Note that Table 8.3 provides an extensive disengagement items checklist.

8.3.1 Contract assessment

First in the series of assessments that we recommend take place is the review of the current contract to ensure all options are catered for:

- Extension clauses.
  Are there agreed extension terms and conditions or do these have to be negotiated? What are the obligations of the parties with regard to extensions? Is there a pre-defined extension period? Is there a pre-agreed pricing provision or is it at the same pricing as normal operations?

End of Contract - Processes

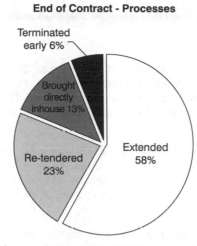

Terminated early 6%

Brought directly inhouse 13%

Re-tendered 23%

Extended 58%

Source: Cullen et al (2001) 51 respondents

End of Contract - Supplier Decisions

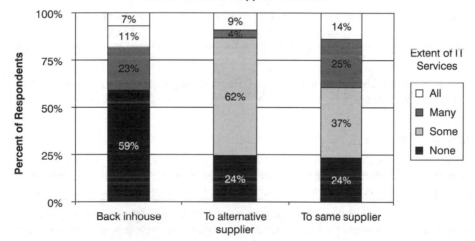

Extent of IT Services

☐ All
■ Many
☐ Some
■ None

Source: Cullen et al (2001) 51 respondents

Figure 8.2 End of contract decisions

- Termination and handover assistance clauses.
  Are there agreed termination and handover terms and conditions or do these have to be negotiated? Are the obligations of all the parties (new supplier, former supplier and the customer organization) with regard to termination and handover complete? Are there pre-defined termination and handover periods? Are there pre-agreed termination and handover pricing provisions or is it at the same pricing as normal operations?

Table 8.3 Disengagement assistance checklist

Fundamentals

❑ Have the parties agreed that disengagement assistance must be conducted such that the business of the organization is able to continue to operate in such a way that services are provided to the organization as if the termination circumstances and resultant disengagement had not occurred and a successor (either the organization or its nominee) is able to continue providing services without interruption?

❑ Does the supplier have the obligation to provide all reasonable disengagement assistance to the organization in the orderly transfer of the disengaged services, functions and operations provided pursuant to the contract to another supplier or to the organization itself during the disengagement period to support the organization's requirements for business continuity during the disengagement?

❑ Does the organization have the right to audit compliance with the disengagement plan and the transition-out provisions in the contract?

❑ Is the supplier required to continue providing the services as per normal operations during the disengagement period?

❑ Does the organization have the right to complete or engage a third party to complete any part of the services taken out of the supplier's hands prior to the termination date and suspend payments otherwise due to the supplier whilst the organization performs or procures the performance of services?

❑ Is there an obligation by the supplier to cease accessing any of the organization's systems including communication links, except with the consent of the organization?

Disengagement plan

❑ Is there a disengagement plan containing full details of the procedures, processes, responsibilities and obligations that arise after a party gives a notice of termination or upon expiry of a term? If not, is there a responsibility of the supplier to provide such a plan?

❑ Is there a description of all things necessary or desirable to conduct the disengagement as efficiently and effectively as possible (including as a result of reviewing the implementation plan to develop a list of those things the parties did at the start of the contract to effect the contract)?

❑ Are there details of the workforce and other resources that will provide disengagement assistance?

❑ Is there an agreed timetable and process for conducting the disengagement?

❑ Is there a schedule of rates to be applicable during the disengagement period and the post-termination period?

Duty for supplier to assist

❑ Is there an duty for the supplier to assist in any tender process conducted for the provision of the disengaged services including base cost models, performance histories and other information concerning the disengaged services and compliance with the SLA?

❑ Is there an obligation by the supplier to review all procedures and software with the new contractor and/or the organization?

Table 8.3 continued

❏ Is there an obligation by the supplier to provide the organization or a replacement supplier with access to all necessary information relevant to the ongoing provision of similar services?

❏ Is the new supplier and/or the organization allowed access to the supplier's site where relevant to assist in the orderly handover?

❏ Is there an obligation by the supplier to be able to novate, assign or procure the novation or assignment of such available software which has become incorporated in the services to the organization to the extent the relevant licensor (if any) allows the supplier to do so, in the form in which it is utilized within the services?

Deliver up

❏ Is there an obligation for the supplier to 'deliver up' all:

- backup in a form reasonably requested by the customer together with any medium containing or capable of reproducing that backup;
- material (electronic and paper based) forms of the organization's confidential information; data, records, documents, drawings, etc in the form required by the organization;
- documents that are necessary to enable services similar to the services to be provided by the organization or its nominee in a manner which ensures orderly transition and continuity of service;
- assets and property owned by the organization in the custody, control or possession of the supplier?

❏ Is there an obligation by the supplier return or (if requested by the organization) destroy any of the organization's confidential information together with any reproduction of that information and any medium containing or capable of reproducing that information?

Post-termination assistance

❏ Is there an obligation for the supplier, subsequent to the disengagement period, to provide to the organization, as necessary:

- answering questions regarding the services on an 'as needed' basis;
- turning over of any remaining organization owned reports and documentation still in the supplier's possession;
- providing the organization with access to all necessary information relevant to the ongoing provision of the disengaged services;
- arranging or procuring the secondment of its workforce as are reasonably required by the organization subject to payment for those workforce the pre-agreed rates; and
- providing access to any information and records in connection with any litigation to which the organization is a party.

❏ Is there an obligation by the supplier to ensure that the data that is relevant to the ongoing provision of the disengaged services are accurate and up to date or to undertake, to the extent that it is unable to comply taking into consideration the condition of the date at the commencement date, to procure for the organization such replacement data as necessary to ensure compliance or alternative to pay the organization the reasonable costs of doing so?

- Post-termination assistance clauses.
  Are there agreed post-termination terms and conditions or do these have to be negotiated? Are the obligations of the former suppler with regard to post-termination complete? Is there a pre-defined post-termination period? Are there pre-agreed post-termination pricing provisions or is it at the same pricing as normal operations?

- Staff and asset 'transfer back' clauses and cost schedule for resources transferred to the incumbent supplier that the organization may want to transfer back.
  Are there agreed transfer back terms and conditions or do these have to be negotiated? Are the obligations of the former supplier with regard to transfer back complete? Is there a pre-defined transfer back offer period? Are there pre-agreed transfer back cost provisions?

For all items that require negotiation, we recommend developing a negotiation strategy (Building Block 5 – 'Commercial mating: select the supplier(s)') to ensure a successful outcome as the former supplier may behave opportunistically.

8.3.2 Whole-of-life arrangement assessment

The next series of assessments cover reviews over the whole-of-life arrangement:

- Conduct a gap analysis between the governing documents and actual operations.
  Unless the parties have been quite diligent in keeping the governing documents (contract, SLA and procedure manuals) up-to-date, these documents are unlikely to be an accurate reflection of the current actual practices and agreements that have evolved over time. This can be seen in the following case study of a government agency.

Case Study: a government agency

The agency was preparing to re-tender a contract near the end of its term. No major changes were believed to be necessary as the intent of the re-tender was for the same scope of services. The re-tender project manager reviewed the contract and SLA expecting that some minor changes might be required, and only gave himself a few days to finalize the new documents. However, he soon found that the contract bore little resemblance to the arrangement currently in operation. A pre-tender update project was required, delaying the tender by months.

- Determine the level of stakeholder satisfaction with the incumbent supplier.
  This is more than a user satisfaction survey. It includes all aspects of the supplier's service delivery, contract, relationship and cost management.

- Analyse performance and cost trends to determine overall value for money since inception.
  In addition to demonstrating the business case for the original outsourcing, the analysis provides the new base case for the future options. It also provides the data for benchmarking and for determining potential improvements in the value for money equation (better KPIs, lower costs).

- Conduct a SWOT (strengths, weaknesses, opportunities and threats).
  This analysis is designed to determine improvements desired in all aspects of the future arrangement, including the contract/SLA, supplier characteristics, scope of services, the contract management function, the retained organization, etc.

- Determine the degree to which the original objectives for outsourcing were achieved.
  This refers to the original business case, and in particular the strategic and tactical purposes the outsourcing arrangement was designed to achieve. This is not always easy, as the following case study reveals.

Case Study: an educational institution

Nearing the end of a five-year contract, the Chancellor of a university directed the Contract Manager to assess whether or not the benefits sought by outsourcing were achieved. This analysis was critical to forming part of the steering committee's strategic planning over whether further outsourcing should be considered. No documentation other than the original contract had been maintained and none of the decision makers or even personnel involved with the outsourcing process remained with the university. Although a valiant effort was made, the Contract Manager could not infer what benefits were intended let alone whether they were achieved.

8.3.3 Knowledge refreshment assessment

It is inevitable that industry and outsourcing practices in general will have evolved since the original arrangement was put in place. The end of any outsourcing contract offers the opportunity to investigate and adopt evolved practices, particularly if this had not been an ongoing inherent process adopted by the organization's contract management function.

This assessment is identical to those conducted in Building Block 1 – 'Discard the myths: gather acumen'.

- Benchmark performance levels and cost against comparative industry standards to determine if KPIs should be upgraded, and to determine future cost expectations.
  Have new KPIs for the services emerged in the market? Are the service levels in the current arrangement appropriate or have new industry standards emerged? Have prices gone up or down for similar scope?

- Update knowledge of leading practice.
  Is there new technology that offers better price/performance ratios? Have new business processes been adopted that offer improved effectiveness or efficiency? Are there better outsourcing and retained organization practices that have emerged in other organizations? Is there new best practice in outsourcing contracts and SLAs?

- Determine the pool of potential suppliers.
  What is the new degree of competitiveness in the industry? Are there any new entrants to be considered? What is the viability and organizational landscape for the 'known' suppliers? Are there any windows of opportunities (i.e. a market slump, a new entrant)? Are there windows of 'dis-opportunities' (i.e. competing tenders from other organizations)?

8.3.4 New requirements assessment

The end of any outsourcing contract offers the opportunity to determine new requirements and refresh original requirements, particularly if this had not been an ongoing inherent process adopted by the organization's contract management function.

This assessment is identical to those conducted in the Architect Phase: Building Blocks 2, 3, and 4:

- Building Block 2 – Prepare strategies: forecast business requirements and potential changes over the projected life of any new/revised arrangement.
- Building Block 3 – Target services: reconsider the scope, potential bundling/unbundling of services and services that should be discontinued, and prepare the target services profiles.
- Building Block 4 – Design future: develop revised SLA(s), contract and price model in addition to the contract management function and the retained organization.

8.3.5 Options assessment

Prepare the options analysis to:

- determine the viability and potential costs, benefits and risks of transacting and managing each option;
- develop the business case and strategy for the recommended option.

Depending on how the organization chooses to progress, it could go through the outsourcing lifecycle in its entirety, should it wish to re-tender a much wider scope of services, or just continue with contract management if it decides to rollover on the same terms and conditions. All three options – re-tender, backsource, retain – take a different path through the lifecycle once the first four building blocks have been conducted (see Figure 8.3).

If the incumbent supplier is to be retained, the contract should be re-negotiated to reflect the organization's changed requirements and improvements in outsourcing practices – thus the lifecycle continues at Building Block 5 ('Commercial mating: select the supplier(s)') with the negotiation strategy. However, if no major changes are required the contract can be renewed following the standard contractual variation processes – thus the

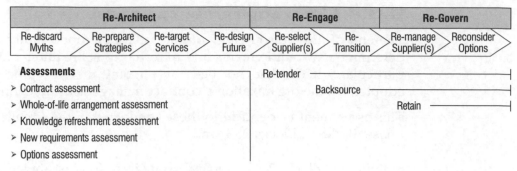

Figure 8.3 Options and the outsourcing lifecycle

lifecycle continues at Building Block 7 ('Get the results: manage the ITO') with the variations strategy.

If the contract is to be re-tendered, the lifecycle continues at Building Block 5 with the selection stages and strategy, albeit more efficiently based on the learning curve from the previous arrangement.

If the services are to be brought in-house, or 'backsourced,' the lifecycle continues at Building Block 6 ('The starting gate: make the transition') with the transition strategy. The contract management function, as the primary source of expertise regarding the previous arrangement, should assist with the transition and investment requirements. Ideally, the SLA will remain to guide and measure service delivery for those services backsourced, although the contract is unlikely to be needed unless the backsourced supplier is a related entity rather than an in-house service unit.

When faced with a re-tender or backsourcing as the preferred option, many organizations regret the lack of knowledge they have over the detailed operations of the supplier's service provision. This is the result of abdicating certain responsibilities, namely ensuring enough knowledge is maintained to facilitate the options, making possible a handover and ensuring that the service is portable. Look at the following case study, for an example.

Case Study: a logistics corporation

The first responsibility of the new IT manager for a port logistics company was to conduct a tender for the IT network management services as the current five-year contract was expiring shortly. He awarded a contract to a new supplier that had offered a price that was 80% less than any other bid. The contract was awarded quickly to lock in that price. Unfortunately, he had poorly specified the nature of the services because he was unfamiliar with the services and did not have appropriate technical expertise. The new supplier's bid was irrelevant as compared to the actual nature of the services required and grossly under-scoped. Furthermore, the new supplier did not have the expertise to conduct the scope of the required services. The incumbent supplier was hired back at premium prices as the organization did not have the time to go through another tender and needed the services operational immediately.

8.4 Preparing for a handover from an incumbent supplier

The handover process from one supplier to another (be the new supplier external or internal) is fraught with inherent difficulties because there is often little incentive for the former supplier to ensure the process is thorough and comprehensive.

Many of the problems associated with handovers between suppliers, which are difficult to begin with, are because the organization failed to:

- require appropriate termination and handover obligations on the part of the former supplier in the contract, thus having to pay premium prices for assistance, recreate intellectual property owned by the supplier, and handover incomplete documentation, even incomplete systems;
- specify appropriate handover procedures and obligations of the new supplier in the re-tender, thus having extensive out-of-scope charges applied; and/or
- require, as part of the re-tender bid response, the detailed handover approach by the new supplier, thus having a faulty handover process and delayed normal operations.

Many organizations assume that any new supplier will have thorough handover procedures and do little in the way of due diligence to ensure that the procedures will be effective, thus abdicating their responsibility to ensure the handover will be successful. Remember, however, that it is predominately in the customer's best interest to ensure the handover is as smooth as possible, not necessarily in either supplier's interests.

The former supplier may have some motivation to retain goodwill, but this can be exhausted quickly. The new supplier has similar motivation to create goodwill with the organization, but will have many opportunities to obtain out-of-scope charges if its obligations have not been specified, or the former supplier does not perform its obligations to the required extent. Relying on the assumption that either supplier will act in the customer's best interest is a high-risk strategy. Some of these difficulties can be read into the following case study.

Case Study: a water utility

A contract was awarded to a new supplier for relatively complex services. The new supplier did not have any handover procedures, nor were they asked to provide any by the customer organization. The handover meeting with the former supplier took 15 minutes and was comprised of a brief conversation whereby the new supplier asked what the former had prepared for them. The former supplier just gave an overview of the configuration, although it had prepared other items at quite length in anticipation of an extensive handover process. Over the course of the next six months, there were so many repeated operational failures that the systems were exceedingly unstable. Accordingly, the customer threatened to sue the new supplier for breach of contract. The new supplier, in turn, threatened to sue the former supplier. The former supplier was able to prove to the customer that it had left an effectively operating environment and through its comprehensive backup was able to restore the system as at the handover date. The new supplier had to pick up the costs of the restoration and of the re-entry of six months company data, which were significant. It spent the remainder of the contract attempting to recoup those costs through out-of-scope charges.

There are certain basic steps necessary to ensure a smooth transition between suppliers:

1 Electronic snapshots of departed operations – sealed, dated and stored (potentially in escrow if desirable):
   - comprehensive backup of all data and systems at handover date including at least one year of history;
   - photographs of operations centre;
   - key documentation including network maps, configuration, systems software, etc.
2 Detailed plans – agreed between all parties:
   - comprehensive project plan and list of tasks;
   - responsibility assignment matrix;
   - test and acceptance procedures and approvals;
   - contingency and restoration plans.
3 Active management – by all parties:
   - a steering committee or oversight board comprised of key organizational personnel;
   - a handover management team comprised of all parties;
   - joint problem solving workshops and planning sessions.

Preparing for termination, handover to another supplier, or bringing an IT activity back in-house – all these can seem a very long way off when an organization is still at the highly promising stage of being about to sign what looks like a win–win contract. However, all contracts do terminate, and it can only be good management practice to ensure that there is as little devil in the detail of termination as there should be in the basic terms of the more active service arrangement with a supplier.

Information technology outsourcing can deliver benefits to any organization, but these benefits are not inherent in the act of outsourcing. Outsourcing is not a transaction led by a contract. Rather, it is an ongoing commercial relationship supported by a number of governance mechanisms, of which one is the contract.

To realize the full value that outsourcing can provide, the need to become an informed purchaser, to plan and design the commercial arrangement, to carefully select the best value-for-money supplier, and to put in the appropriate management skills and effort – all these are paramount.

These building blocks have been designed to ensure organizations do just that. They set out the issues and recommended processes. We have concentrated on helping organizations by pinpointing where things have gone wrong, in our experience, over the last two decades, and what the remedies have been. Our overwhelming finding over the years has been that thorough preparation and strongly resourced management does make a significant difference in the results you can expect to get from outsourcing.

Below are some of the key principles we have extracted from this book. An organization can never have enough hindsight, if it can be translated into intelligent, pre-emptive foresight.

Accountability In no event can the organization's ultimate accountability for the success of IT be abdicated. Strategic flaws cannot be sold off.

Contracts There is no standard outsourcing contract, only headings. Go through the issues in considerable detail. But make the contract usable.

Cost   The lowest price can be the highest cost. ITO is not an auction – get the best price with a superior supplier under a fair agreement with sustainable solutions.

Employee relations   Outsourcing is emotional; manage the FUD factor – fear, uncertainty and doubt.

Negotiating   Post-tender negotiation should only be on exact wording – never on intent or design of the arrangement. Do not hand over a cheque and then decide what you have purchased.

On-going management   Outsourcing does not imply less effort, only a different emphasis.

Outcomes   Outsourcing has been claimed to be able to achieve many things (the honeymoon). Outsourcing has been blamed for many things as well (the backlash). Realize that the claims are not inherent with the act of outsourcing itself, but how the ITO lifecycle has been managed specific to each organization and supplier.

Partnering   Requires significant investment; it is not an opportunity for shortcuts, or abandoning responsibility to the supplier.

Performance measurement   People and suppliers manage according to what they are measured and incentivized by. The existence of a contract alone will not ensure performance.

Planning   Ignorance is not bliss – what you don't know and haven't planned for will hurt you.

Strategy   Outsourcing is a strategy, not an economy. Do not be tempted to obtain perceived advantages with a poorly thought out strategy. For each advantage outsourcing provides there is a disadvantage and vice versa – identify and manage both.

Win–win   Not just a good idea. The result of thorough preparation, shared information, engaged, skilled management on both sides, and respect for each other's objectives.

References and Brief Further Reading

Cullen, S., Willcocks, L. and Seddon, P. (2001). *Information Technology Outsourcing Practices in Australia*. Deloitte Touche Tohmatsu, Melbourne.

Feeny, D. (1997). Information systems organization: the role of users and specialists. In: Willcocks, L., Feeny, D. and Iseli, G. (eds). *Managing IT as a Strategic Resource*. McGraw-Hill, Maidenhead.

Kern, T. and Willcocks, L. (2001). *The Relationship Advantage: Information Technologies, Sourcing and Management*. Oxford University Press, Oxford.

Kern, T., Lacity, M. and Willcocks, L. (2002a). *Netsourcing: Renting Applications and Services Over a Network*. FT/Prentice Hall, New York.

Kern, T., Willcocks, L. and Van Heck, E. (2002b). The winner's curse in IT outsourcing: strategies for avoiding relational trauma. *California Management Review* **44**(2): 47–69.

Lacity, M. and Hirschheim, R. (1995). *Beyond the Information Systems Outsourcing Bandwagon*. Wiley, Chichester.

Lacity, M. and Willcocks, L. (2000). *Inside Information Technology Outsourcing: A State of the Art Report*. Templeton Executive Research Briefing, Templeton College, Oxford.

Lacity, M. and Willcocks, L. (2001). *Global Information Technology Outsourcing: In Search of Business Advantage*. Wiley, Chichester.

Loh, Lawrence and Venkatraman, N. (1992). Diffusion of information technology outsourcing influence sources and the Kodak Effect. *Information Systems Research* December, 334–358.

Seddon, P., Cullen, S. and Willcocks, L. (2002). Does Domberger's theory of the contracting organization apply to IT outsourcing? In: *Proceedings of the International Conference in Information Systems*. Barcelona, December 16–18th.

Willcocks, L. and Greaser, V. (2000). *Delivering IT and E-Business Value*. Butterworth-Heinemann, Oxford.

Willcocks, L., Petherbridge, P. and Olson, N. (2002). *Making IT Count: Strategy, Delivery, Infrastructure*. Butterworth-Heinemann, Oxford.

Index